an evil outfit of crazed scholars set out to create a new diction- ary of misspelled words. Their goal was to create chaos, wreak havoc, and confuse all students everywhere. By creat- ing thousands of mutant mis- spelled words, these evildoers hoped to doom students, writers, test-takers, and acade- micians from every corner of the universe. Unfortunately, these scholars released the mutants and rogues from their lab of terror and sent the menacing hordes straight to Earth. Laughing evil laughs, the demon words hurled them- selves across the universe, quickly landing in books and spell checks everywhere. As the fate of universal spelling hangs in the balance, we find that there's only one who is capable of delivering us from the evil scholars' handiwork:

HER NAME IS . . .

CHI

Avalon

Get Wise!
MASTERING
SPELLING
SKILLS

By Nathan Barber

THOMSON

PETERSON'S

Australia • Canada • Mexico • Singapore • Spain • United Kingdom • United States

THOMSON
PETERSON'S

I wish I were a superhero . . .

Get Wise! Mastering Spelling Skills
ISBN: 0-7689-1244-X

Printed in Canada

10 9 8 7 6 5 4 3 2 1   05 04 03

First Edition

Acknowledgments

Thanks first and foremost to Christy and Noah for being willing to see me only over my laptop screen for as long as it took to do this project.

A huge thanks to Laurie Barnett for her ideas, her direction, and for thinking of me for this project. An even bigger thanks to Laurie for never E-Zapping me!

Finally, here's to whoever it was that beat me in the junior high spelling bee back in the day!

Contents

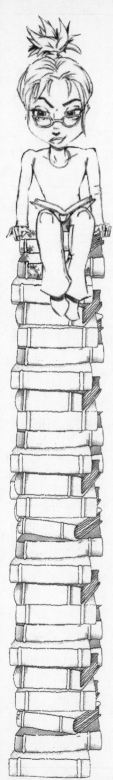

Gear up and join Chi on all 30 levels as you destroy the mutant words and neutralize the enemy. The world balance is in your hands . . .

Introduction

Thankfully, we rescued this manuscript from the clutches of a little old lady who taught spelling back in the 1930s. We have since reassigned her to *Get Wise! Mastering Knitting Skills*. Contrary to what she thinks, spelling doesn't have to be so bad. It can actually be fun! Hey, we've been in your shoes, and we know that spending extra time learning how to spell may not be your first choice about what to do with your time. That's why we promise we'll make this as painless as we can. But you've got to be open-minded, because we have some pretty unusual exercises in the pages ahead!

Maybe your mom or dad bought this book for you because you kept leaving notes on the refrigerator that said:

I wint to the librery to study for my trygonomitry test.
Be back later.

Or maybe your significant other bought this book for you because your last love letter said:

You now, this weekend is hour fith month anniversery
and I think we should do something spesial.

We hope you saw the humor here. However, even if you didn't get the point, you've still have come to the right place! There were tons of misspelled words in those examples. Some of the misspelled words were pretty easy words, and some were more challenging. Bottom line, misspelled words are misspelled words!

Maybe when you first got this book you thought, "Why do I need a spelling book? Spelling isn't that important! Besides, I always let my computer do a spell check for me." Spelling is actually very important, and just like in the examples above, you won't always have access to a computer to check your spelling. There will actually be times when you'll have to write things down with an old-fashioned pen and paper! That's so low-tech, but that's just the way it is!

You're probably wondering how we plan to make a spelling book nonpainful and perhaps even fun. Well, we have a two-pronged plan of attack. First, this book will actually turn into a video game complete with sound effects, high-tech digital images, holographs, and more! You'll see what we mean when we get into Chapter 1, or rather Level 1. Second, we have enlisted the help of one of the universe's greatest adventurers: Chi. Ever heard of Xena? Lara Croft? They have nothing on Chi.

So, without further *adieu*, allow us to introduce you to the Word Warrior, the Splendid Speller, the Verbose Vixen, the First Lady of Loquacity, Chi!

Huh . . .

After all that hype, that's all you have to say? How anticlimactic is that?

Hey . . . What's this weird outfit you've got me in? *Really* uncomfortable, totally *last century* . . . how many people are going to see me in this!

Well, perhaps you didn't read the fine print on your contract Chi, but this is part of the deal. And last time I looked, there weren't too many spelling books on the best seller list, so no need to worry too much. But we *are* relying on you to get us all through a number of perilous levels that we'll need to complete before we are finished.

That darn small print! You should see what they had me wearing in *Get Wise! History.* Oh well, all in a day's work.

Before we jump to the first level, let's go over a few basic things. These tips will be like your instruction manual or survival guide for the video game. First, find a quiet place to work through this book and set aside about ten or fifteen minutes a day to commit to improving your spelling. That's all you'll need to be a much better speller…with the help of Chi, of course! Second, you'll need a pen or pencil for some of the levels, so always have one handy. Third, there are 30 levels and they must be completed in order. Any variance from the predetermined order could spell disaster for the universe (get it?) Finally, be brave! You'll be able to handle anything the game throws at you! If you're ready, then let's get started. Chi? Your line.

Uh, yeah, right . . . Please advance to Level 1?

Sounds good! See you there!

Level 1

Battle of the E-Zappers

Before we get started with Level 1, we have to break some bad news to you. The publisher slashed our budget to practically nothing. Remember those sound effects and digital images we promised? Gone. Remember the holographic images? Gone. We barely have enough left in our budget to afford Chi, but we knew we couldn't get by without her.

> **You got that right! But no cool lights and sounds and stuff? So now what am I going to do? Don't I need some kind of weapon or gadgetry if I am going to … save the universe … from … uh, what, spelling destruction?**

Yes, the battle must go on, and we do indeed have a very interesting array of "gadgetry" for you, starting with a very special writing implement. In fact, as the chapter title indicates, we're starting you off with the "E-Zapper"! But we guess you'll just have to make up your own sound effects, and as for the lights, you can just read under a disco ball or a strobe light. But let's not dwell on that. Let's get on to Level 1: Battle of the E-Zappers!

Here's the scenario. Somewhere deep in space in a dark laboratory, cruel scholars have added the suffix **-ABLE** to words without removing the silent **E**, which is incorrect, thereby creating our first encounter with "mutant" words.

★ **When the suffix -ABLE is added to a word that ends with a silent E, the final E is usually eliminated.**

So, armed with only an E-Zapper, your writing implement that is, OK, your pencil, you must zap an **E** from each word in a list of words . . . Chi? I believe you have a line here?

Huh? ... uh ... OK, here goes: The mighty Word Warrior is ready! My E-Zapper is loaded and I'm ready to begin zapping!

Who said that? Did I really just say that?

Following is the first list of mutant words that were released from the laboratory. The mutations have left these words misspelled and the spellings must be corrected. Otherwise, these mutant words will creep into papers, tests, letters, and stories everywhere causing incomprehensible mayhem. You must use your E-Zapper to carefully eliminate the silent **E** in each of the following words. Then, rewrite the word correctly in the blank next to it. The first one has been E-Zapped for you.

PLEASUREABLE   <u>PLEASURABLE</u>

DESIREABLE

LIKEABLE

BELIEVEABLE

ADVISEABLE

LIVEABLE

VALUEABLE

ARGUEABLE

USEABLE

EXCUSEABLE

ADMIREABLE

PROVEABLE

LOVEABLE

DEBATEABLE

MOVEABLE

Look how many of those words could describe me: likable, lovable, admirable, valuable, and desirable— that's me!

Congratulations! Your mission has been completed with minimal casualties and difficulty. However, new interstellar intelligence has just learned that the evil scholars in the far-off laboratory didn't mutate *all* the words with suffixes in the same way. Fortunately for you, intelligence has discovered a pattern among the mutated words!

★ **When a word ends in -CE or -GE, the final E must be preserved at all costs before adding -ABLE.**

Keep that in mind as you try the next word list.

Those dastardly evildoers! They're trying to confuse us, but these mutant words are no match for Chi the Word Warrior!

Here is the newest list of mutant words released by the lab. These words have been screened once, but you should probably screen them again to make sure that none of the words from the first list found their way into this list. Read each of the following words and notice that you'll need to *add* an **E** to most of the words.

Uh oh ... so what do I do with my E-Zapper now? Seems to have lost its functionality.

Nope. Now you simply turn your E-Zapper around and backward to *add* an
E instead of zapping it. However, if by some chance, you find a mutant word
from the other list and need to zap it, turn your weapon around again, face it
forward, and zap it immediately! We've done the first one for you.

Cool! Love those reversible, 2-in-1 weapons!

CHANGABLE (E inserted ^)   CHANGEABLE _____

MANAGABLE   _____

ENFORCABLE   _____

NOTICABLE   _____

REPLACABLE   _____

KNOWLEDGABLE   _____

EXCHANGABLE   _____

EXCUSEABLE   _____

TRACABLE   _____

SERVICABLE   _____

**Aha! One of those mutants tried to sneak in but we
got it! It would have been *inexcusable* for it to slip
past our defenses!**

Nice work! You've courageously tackled 24 mutants so far! Before we engage the mutants once more and advance to Level 2, let's review the information we've gathered from our intelligence agents.

★ If a word ends in **-CE** or **-GE,** the silent **E** must be *preserved* when adding **-ABLE.** If a word has any other consonant besides **C** or **G** before the silent **E,** the silent **E** must be *zapped* before adding **-ABLE.**

Before we can advance to Level 2, we must arrange the words from our two lists in alphabetical order. Rewrite the two lists from pages 3 and 5 into one list that is arranged in alphabetical order. You can advance to Level 2 only after successfully completing Level 1. Use the spaces provided below to organize your list. When you have compiled your list, check your list against the answer key in the Appendix.

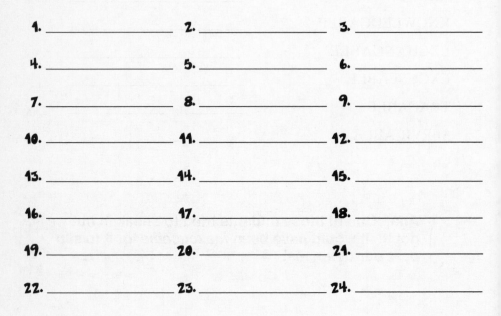

1. _____ 2. _____ 3. _____

4. _____ 5. _____ 6. _____

7. _____ 8. _____ 9. _____

10. _____ 11. _____ 12. _____

13. _____ 14. _____ 15. _____

16. _____ 17. _____ 18. _____

19. _____ 20. _____ 21. _____

22. _____ 23. _____ 24. _____

The Word Warrior has triumphed and reigns supreme as the greatest E-Zapper in the universe! Not so fast ... Just wait until Level 2!

Level 2

Battle of the E-Zappers, Part 2

We've just received new intelligence that the same evil laboratory has now released *hordes* of other mutant words! Thankfully, our intelligence has learned that the only rule you need to remember was already revealed in Level 1.

So, if you encounter *any* of the following suffixes, you are going to zap the silent **E** at the end of the word.

-ER	**-OR**	**-ING**	**-ED**	**-AL**
-IBLE	**-ANCE**	**-ION**	**-OUS**	

Remember: The **-CE, -GE** rule (see page 4) *only* applies to our original suffix, **-ABLE**. In the heat of battle you must remember which **E** to zap and which to preserve!

Those wicked villains! We'll spoil their evil plan! Bring on the mutants!

Following is a list of mutant words that have been rounded up and are ready for E-Zapping. As you did in Level 1, use your E-Zapper to carefully eliminate the silent **E** in each of the words on page 10. Then, rewrite the word correctly in the blank next to it. The first one has been E-Zapped for you.

My E-Zapper is locked, loaded, and ready for elimination!

ACHEING	_ACHING_
SEVEREITY	_____
USEING	_____
REVERSEIBLE	_____
CONFUSEION	_____
ARRIVEAL	_____
COMPLETEING	_____
ACHIEVEING	_____
ADVISEOR	_____
GUIDEANCE	_____
AMUSEING	_____
RESEMBLEANCE	_____
PROPOSEAL	_____
IGNITEION	_____
REHEARSEAL	_____

You have now added fifteen more words to the growing list of words, uh mutants, you have E-Zapped into compliance. Great work! Now rewrite the list from above into a list arranged in alphabetical order and zap any silent **E** that must be eliminated. This will help *confirm* the correct spelling of each.

Sorry, we need to do this twice. Otherwise, the words could turn back into their original mutant forms! After you make your list, check it against the list in the Appendix.

1. _____ 2. _____ 3. _____

4. _____ 5. _____ 6. _____

7. _____ 8. _____ 9. _____

10. _____ 11. _____ 12. _____

13. _____ 14. _____ 15. _____

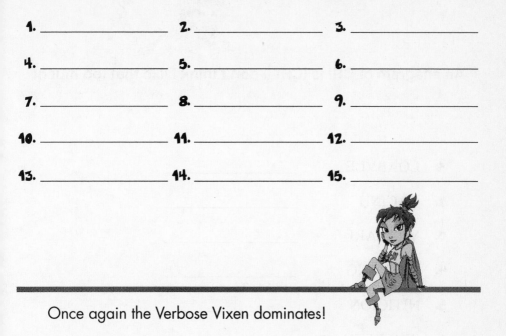

Once again the Verbose Vixen dominates!

Great work again! However, before you can advance to Level 3, you must complete a challenge. You must solve a number of *word scrambles* using the words from Levels 1 and 2. For example, SPELLING becomes LINPLEGS or HARD WORK becomes DHAR ROWK. On the next page, you will see seven word scrambles. You will need to unscramble the word and write it down in the blank next to it. However, make sure all the necessary **E**s have been eliminated. Check your answers against the answer key in the Appendix.

When a word scramble actually creates a new word, we call that an *anagram*. For example, *ear* is an anagram for *are*.

An anagram of CHI is ICH! I don't think I like that too much!

1. LOABVLE _____

2. GACINH _____

3. VRALARI _____

4. MUSAING _____

5. NITIGION _____

6. SIVERETY _____

7. LORPSARP _____

The DROW IRRORWA has prevailed yet again! ICH is invincible! You may now proceed to Level 3.

Level 3

The INpostors

Just when you thought it was safe … The intelligence agents have just reported several *in*postors creeping about and causing problems for spellers.

> Uh oh! It looks like the author of the book may have been *im*fected by the rogues! The word is spelled *im*poster, not *in*poster!

Actually, I was undercover for a moment in case any of those mad scholars were watching me. However, Chi, the correct spelling is *in*fected, not *im*fected!

Don't worry, Chi. We've figured out the antidote! Here's the deal: Apparently, some rogue prefixes are attacking innocent prefixes, assuming their identities! According to reports, the prefixes that are being targeted are **IN-** and **CON-**.

It's *im*conceivable to think these *in*postors will get away with such identity theft!

It seems like we have to move more quickly here. Chi, check your spelling! According to the rules of spelling:

★ **IN-** and **CON-** are prefixes for all words except those beginning with **B, M,** and **P.**

★ For words beginning with **B, M,** and **P,** the prefixes **IM-** and **COM-** step in.

It seems the verbal powers-that-be that assembled the words in the English language took pity on our tongues and created prefix rules that form the easiest words for us to say. For example, isn't it just easier, and doesn't it just sound better to say **IMMEDIATE** rather than **INMEDIATE**, or **COMPETITION** instead of **CONPETITION**?

The masterminds behind the savage attacks on these prefixes, however, would rather have everyone in the universe confused, especially when it comes to spelling. The intelligence community has been working overtime to identify particular words that have needlessly suffered at the hands of the rogue prefixes. A number of those words have been collected, debriefed, and compiled in a list for you. The only task left is to replace the false letters with the true letters in the prefixes. The faulty letters have been surgically removed, and now survival will depend on your ability to restore the prefixes, and thus the words, to their original state. In the following blanks, fill in the correct letter. Refer back to the rules about **IN-** and **IM-** and **CON-** and **COM-** if you need help completing this exercise. We've already done the first one for you.

> I was *com*fused for a moment there, but now I'm ready for *in*mediate action! Do I sound like an *in*becile?

CO _N_ GRESSIONAL

I__MORTALITY

CO__PROMISE

I__MUNITY

I__NOCENT

CO__SERVATIVE

I__TUITION

I__BEDDED

CO__NOTATION

CO__MENTATOR

I__MEDIATELY

I__PATIENT

I__MACULATE

I__SULATION

CO__BUSTION

CO__PETITION

CO__MERCIAL

I__POSTOR

I__PEACH

Excellent work! Nineteen new words have been liberated! That's great news for millions of readers and students everywhere. We knew we could count on you! Apparently you took advantage of the info that was collected.

The fate of the universe, or at least a few of the words in the universe, depends on your finding all the perilous prefixes. Refer back to the list on the previous page and write the words in alphabetical order. When you finish, compare your list to the list in the Appendix.

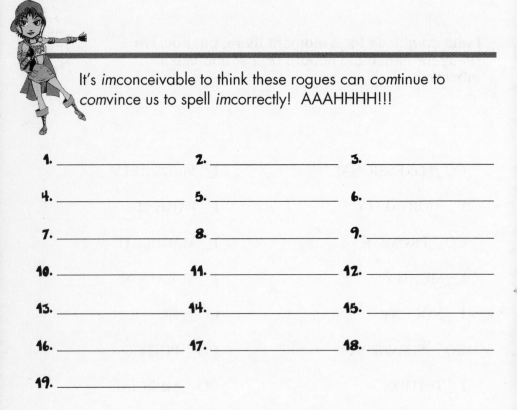

It's *im*conceivable to think these rogues can *com*tinue to *com*vince us to spell *im*correctly! AAAHHHH!!!

1. _____ 2. _____ 3. _____

4. _____ 5. _____ 6. _____

7. _____ 8. _____ 9. _____

10. _____ 11. _____ 12. _____

13. _____ 14. _____ 15. _____

16. _____ 17. _____ 18. _____

19. _____

Nice work! Before you can advance to Level 4, though, you have one final task. Apparently the *in*postors have taken the innocent words deep into hiding among not only random letters but also among other *in*postors. You must find ten of the words from the list above hidden somewhere in the chaos that follows. When you find one, circle it with your writing implement. Be sure to search up, down, forward, backward, and diagonally. Beware of the *in*postors, though!

Level 3 Challenge

Complete the following puzzle challenge by identifying the correctly spelled words from Level 3 in the chaos below. Challenge solutions are in the Appendix.

INPOSTER CHAOS

```
        W F D   B B N U
      C C C R Q I   K H C
    X Q O O Y J H N C O E
  N H T N M M N P N O M F F
  N O I P P P G L D O N N N D
Y I I Q N R E V R I I G O X O E I
B T N T O O O T S G E T R T E I D N W
N I B I I I M I E E N S E A S T D M D
K N E U M T I T T T O U S T I S E U I
F U D T S I S I A A I B S I M U B N T
B M D M U T E O L L T M I O O B M I G
U M E I L E O N U U A O O N R N I T T
X I D O A P Q S C C L C N D P O A Y T
Q T N T N A E A A U O A N M C J L
  J G I O F A M M S A L Q O D F
    L O C I E M N N Q D R C C
    N C A M I I I S L T R
      N O I T I U T N I
        K P F C M J J
```

That was nearly impossible, but with *concentration*, we did it! Hey! I'm fixed now! You may advance to Level 4.

Level 4

The Silence of the Letters: Sychological Warfare

Sometimes the most dangerous enemies are the ones you can't see, and sometimes the most dangerous weapons are those that can't be detected. Such is the case in Level 4. The hordes released onto the unsuspecting world of students have resorted to crimes more cunning than just identity theft and beating up on poor, innocent word parts. According to new intelligence reports, the evil scholars trained a special regiment of secret fighters that specializes in mind games!

These mental warriors have struck at the very heart of the spelling community. Apparently, in the first-known spelling mental attack, the sinister agents targeted a number of words containing *silent letters*. Using top-secret brainwashing techniques, the agents got to certain words and convinced the words to rid themselves of their silent letters! As a result, a number of brainwashed words are now only but shells of their former selves.

Ah, I see what you mean! Our poor little chapter title is missing its **P**.

Yes, and therefore it is of the utmost importance to be familiar with words containing silent letters so that you can still recognize them in their diseased and twisted shape. Fortunately, thanks to extensive archives, we have been able to compile a complete set of the words as they appeared *before the attacks*. In order to familiarize yourself with the words, read through the archived list. As you read each word, circle or underline the silent letter in each word. We've done the first one for you.

Just look at them ... they look so peaceful. Little did they know what horrors were about to be unleashed on them!

DESI<u>G</u>NER   RHAPSODY

ALIGNMENT   RHYME

CAMPAIGN   AUTUMN

GNAW   COLUMN

INDEBTED   RHYTHM

DOUBTFUL   CONDEMN

PSALMS   PLUMB

PSYCHOLOGY   CALM

SPAGHETTI	NUMB
GHETTO	QUALM
SOLEMN	

As you can clearly see in the list above, many words have letters in them that are silent. Contrary to rumors that the villainous warriors are spreading, the silent letters are actually very important for the proper spelling of the words. Your mission is to know how to spell them!

A report has just come in across our server that the brainwashed words have been tracked and spotted. While they are being rounded up, write the list above in alphabetical order. Take careful note of the correct spellings, including, of course, the silent letter in each word. After you compile your list, check it against the list provided in the Appendix.

If we don't get them right in the alphabetical list, it's *doutful* that we'll be able to help these poor words! They'll be *condemed* to permanent misspellings!

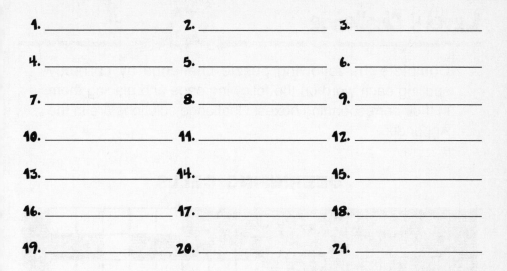

1. _____ 2. _____ 3. _____

4. _____ 5. _____ 6. _____

7. _____ 8. _____ 9. _____

10. _____ 11. _____ 12. _____

13. _____ 14. _____ 15. _____

16. _____ 17. _____ 18. _____

19. _____ 20. _____ 21. _____

Excellent work! You finished the list just in the nick of time! Our field agents have rescued the words in the list above. Now it will be your job to successfully *debrief* the words. To debrief them, remove the misspelled words from the list on page 23 and place the new, corrected words in the appropriate Debriefing Cells provided. In order for these words to achieve complete assimilation back into the verbal world, they must be spelled correctly and allowed sufficient time to debrief.

We have to remain *cam* and focused as we perform this *solem* task!

Level 4 Challenge

Complete the following puzzle challenge by correctly spelling each word on the following page and placing them in their corresponding boxes. Challenge solutions are in the Appendix.

DEBRIEFING CELLS

Across

1. quam
3. campain
6. sychology
8. spagetti
9. salms
15. doutful
16. cam
17. num
18. ndeted
19. desiner

Down

2. alinment
4. rythm
5. rapsody
7. naw
9. plum
10. autum
11. solem
12. colum
13. ryme
14. getto
16. condem

Great work! Compare your final work with that in the Appendix. In the time that it takes you to check your work, the words should be debriefed.

Congratulations! You have successfully completed Level 4. You may now advance to Level 5.

Level 5

The Double-Consonant Cloaking Device

Our field agents have just intercepted a top-secret message, which was sent from the infamous deep-space laboratory. As soon as the message is decoded, we can give you instructions concerning your mission for Level 5. Initial reports seem to indicate that the message has something to do with a "cloaking device."

Oh no! I don't know if I remember how to do the Heimlich maneuver!

No, Chi, not a choking device! The report mentioned something about a *cloaking* device! A cloaking device is a high-tech contraption that can render anything invisible. Understand?

Will it work on the blemishes in my oily T-zone?

Get serious, Chi! The report is in, and the outlook is not very good. It seems that the scholars equipped a few agents with cloaking devices, and these agents have targeted certain words containing double consonants. Many words such as:

* ★ SPELLING

* ★ PRETTY

* ★ MESSAGE

* ★ BOTTLE

contain double consonants, but these simple words rarely give spellers any trouble. The cloaking-device-carrying crooks have chosen some more complex words, words that are listed for you on the next page.

The cloaking device is designed to make one consonant in a double-consonant set *completely disappear*. Therefore, when you see the words later on, after they have been struck by the cloaking device, they won't look like they do in our list here. So, your first job is to read through the list and become familiar with the words. We'll look at the cloaking device's carnage later.

<u>INN</u>OCUOUS	ASSASSIN
COLOSSAL	INNUENDO
DISSIPATE	QUESTIONNAIRE
HARASS	TYRANNY
HARASSMENT	BATTALION
NECESSARY	SUFFOCATE
POSSESS	COLLAPSE
POSSESSION	CORRESPOND
ASSESS	OFFICIAL
ASSESSMENT	BROCCOLI
CASSEROLE	SUCCESS

Did you get a good look at these words? Great. Now before we move on, you should probably familiarize yourself with them a little more. Using your writing implement, go back through the list and underline the sets of double consonants. We've done the first one for you.

I feel like I'm seeing double!

That's because you were seeing double, Chi: lots and lots of double consonants. Unfortunately, the list you were working with was a list from *our* archives. The words you saw appeared as they did *before the cloaking-device disaster*. Shortly, you will need to reconstruct the words as they should be, each having at least one set of double consonants. Before you do, arrange the words from our list into an alphabetical list. This will help you remember and visualize the correctly spelled words. When you're done, compare your list with the one in the Appendix.

> **Just think, all those words still think they look normal, but they are actually freakishly misspelled! Poor things!**

1. _____ 2. _____ 3. _____

4. _____ 5. _____ 6. _____

7. _____ 8. _____ 9. _____

10. _____ 11. _____ 12. _____

13. _____ 14. _____ 15. _____

16. _____ 17. _____ 18. _____

19. _____ 20. _____ 21. _____

22. _____

Nice job! You should be pretty familiar by now with the archived file of the double-consonant words. Just in the nick of time, too! Our researchers at the lab have been working overtime on an antidote for the effects of the cloaking, but their efforts have been in vain. At this point, the fate of these words lies solely in the hands of the Word Warrior.

Warning: Before you move on to the list of words that need reconstructive surgery, you should know that what you are about to see may be disturbing. The words have been horribly disfigured by the cloaking device. Take a deep breath; then look at the list. What you will need to do is look at each word one by one. Then, rewrite the word correctly in the space next to it. Hopefully, this will be enough to save these words. To make sure you saved the words, compare your answers with those in the Appendix. We've done the first one for you.

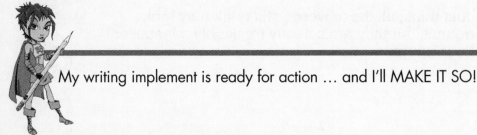

My writing implement is ready for action ... and I'll MAKE IT SO!

INOCUOUS	*INNOCUOUS*	ASASIN	_____
COLOSAL	_____	INUENDO	_____
DISIPATE	_____	QUESTIONAIRE	_____
HARAS	_____	TYRANY	_____
HARASMENT	_____	BATALION	_____
NECESSARY	_____	SUFOCATE	_____
POSES	_____	COLAPSE	_____
POSESION	_____	CORESPOND	_____
ASES	_____	OFICIAL	_____
ASESMENT	_____	BROCOLI	_____
CASEROLE	_____	SUCES	_____

Phew! That was a tough battle there, and I don't know what kind of aftershock I will experience from seeing such horrible misspellings.

Sometimes it seems like there should be *two* sets of double consonants in these kind of words. A few good examples are HARASS, SUFFOCATE, and BROCCOLI. You just have to remember which consonants in those words are doubled. On the other hand, words like ASSASSIN, POSSESS, and ASSESS *do* have two sets of double consonants. Isn't it hard to believe that the cloaking device was so powerful that it zapped both sets in these words? This is no small-time operation that we're up against.

In fact, the cloaking device is so powerful that we still aren't ready to move on to the next level. Our team of surgeons was called in to operate on some of the words that sustained permanent damage. Unfortunately, they weren't able to reconstruct the words. Therefore, in order to advance to Level 6, you must correctly reconstruct the list for them.

On page 30, you will see a list of words. Each of the words has had a letter extracted from it. To complete this level, you must correctly reconstruct the word in the blank next to the word. Be sure you reconstruct each word with the correct set of double consonants. Don't be confused by the extra spaces left in each word by the surgeons who obviously have weaker spelling skills than surgical skills. Only add a consonant where one is needed! Their fates depend on you! After you complete the exercise, compare your results with the list in the Appendix. We've already done the first one for you.

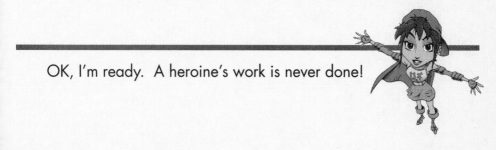

OK, I'm ready. A heroine's work is never done!

1. TYR__AN**N**Y   _TYRANNY_

2. NEC__ES__ARY

3. DIS__IP__ATE

4. BAT__AL__ION

5. IN__O__UOUS

6. COL__OS__AL

7. CAS__ER__OLE

8. QUESTION__AIR__E

Congratulations! You have successfully conquered Level 5. You have reversed the effects of the double-consonant cloaking device . . . at least for now. You may now advance to Level 6.

Level 6

The Attack of the Z-Rays

A new breed of mutants has converged upon the universe, and once again, it will be up to Chi to sort out the mess.

Man, if it isn't my little brother whom I have to clean up after, it's those mutant demon words! Who knows what perils I'll face next?

These new mutants are, of course, more misspelled words, but specifically words ending in **-ISE** and **-IZE**. Masquerading as correctly spelled words, their goal is, of course, mass chaos and confusion! Many students already have difficulty deciding which words should be spelled with **-ISE** and which should be spelled with **-IZE**. These mutants prey on that confusion, indecision, and vulnerability by presenting themselves as **-ISE** words when they should be **-IZE** words and vice versa. They must be stopped at all costs!

But how will we recogn*ise* them?

Chi, I see they've already started their madness and mayhem, and *you* have fallen victim to their trickery! Luckily, our gadget gurus have developed Z-Ray glasses for you. These fancy glasses will give you Z-ray vision, or the ability to see whether or not a word should be spelled with an **S** or a **Z**. Intelligence has compiled a list of likely words to be targeted by the mutants. Try on the glasses, read through the list below, and become familiar with each word:

SUPERVISE	**CRITICIZE**
ADVISE	**AUTHORIZE**
CHASTISE	**SANITIZE**
DESPISE	**VISUALIZE**
IMPROVISE	**CAPSIZE**
EXERCISE	**UTILIZE**
DEVISE	**CAPITALIZE**
REVISE	**ORGANIZE**

ADVERTISE   **AGONIZE**

SURPRISE   **RECOGNIZE**

> Wow! I can see that this is going to be a critical mission! Thank goodness for my new shades!

But if anyone can do it, our Word Warrior can! The first step in outdoing these mutants is becoming more familiar with the targeted words. Just for practice, we have created a list for you, but the **S** and **Z** in each word has been omitted. Fill in the blank inside each word with either an **S** or a **Z** so that the completed word is spelled correctly. When you have finished the training exercise, compare your list with the one provided for you in the Appendix. The first one has been done for you.

CAPITALI_Z_E   CRITICI__E

ADVI__E   ADVERTI__E

CAPSI__E   SANITI__E

UTILI__E   VISUALI__E

IMPROVI__E   CHASTI__E

ORGANI__E   DESPI__E

DEVI__E   SUPERVI__E

REVI__E   EXERCI__E

AUTHORI__E   AGONI__E

SURPRI__E   RECOGNI__E

Very tricky! But I'll get all those mutant words ...
and their little dog, too!

Uh, I think you're thinking about another book, Chi? Now, indeed they can be tricky, but you're starting to get the hang of it. Now that you're becoming more and more familiar with the words that have been targeted by the masquerading makers of mayhem, let's do one more training exercise before we put it all on the line. Rewrite the list on page 33 in alphabetical order, and then compare your list to the list provided for you in the Appendix.

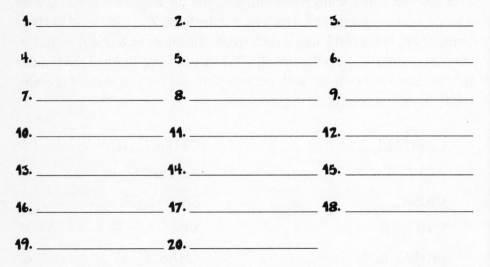

1. _____ 2. _____ 3. _____

4. _____ 5. _____ 6. _____

7. _____ 8. _____ 9. _____

10. _____ 11. _____ 12. _____

13. _____ 14. _____ 15. _____

16. _____ 17. _____ 18. _____

19. _____ 20. _____

Excellent work! It looks like you're ready for the big showdown with the mutants. Here's the situation: The mutants have hidden amongst a number of friendly, correctly spelled words. We can't eliminate the mutants until we correctly identify the normal words. It's up to you to scour the following area for words that are *spelled correctly*. When you find one, circle it with your writing implement. But beware of the mutants! Don't be fooled into circling any of the mutants, or we may have some serious problems later on in our battle against the forces of darkness. Fifteen correctly spelled words are in there somewhere among the mutant mash. Be careful! Be sure to search up,

Get Wise! Mastering Spelling Skills

down, forward, backward, and diagonally. When you've identified all the
friendlies, check your work with the solution in the Appendix.

Level 6 Challenge

Complete the following puzzle challenge by identifying the
15 correctly spelled words. Challenge solutions are in the
Appendix.

MUTANT MASH

```
                            X V X
                        A N E V S E T S X
                    M P X Z G I L H Z N U S I
                M M Q C J E M S E L E I A P H Z S
              Y W X J W R S W U B Z S N N R E O N C
            G H Q P D E S I L A U S I V E A Y R E C H
            B W L Q V T N V T L F T T V U P G I V R Y
            S M K P I B M Y O M I I K I A D V E R T I Z E
            X H A S J U O K R Y Z C Z N K I A A R O T Z L
            I B R E K N T U U P E E E I A S U P E R V I S E
            V Y C P L A P G X M Z         S S E K A N L C N C B
            V P F D D H M S V I           E S I L A T I P A N
          O Y U D I J U P C V             Z B T U J Z E P C U
          D H X S E Z U S O C             M I T T Y E Z S J N
          R D Q T K S P R S T             P I R H G Z I I J Y
          E E K V K P U K R F             A L D Z O B R L S E
          P H S Z M M I H S V J       C I E Z L R H O I E K
          M W T I G B E S I N O G A A S N Z N C I V T T D Q
          Y J W Z G M S E F S Q P E G M I I T S R J U G F
          Q G J R Q Z O Z Z P S O R G A N I S E Q N M A
            G Y H B E E J X I F S A R E O Q V D E O I
            D P F H B V A Z S P H A X L G D G Y D L R
              N Z S Q J E E U E S I V D A A A F Q Q
                B Z R K C A Z M J E P W V V E U T
                  N S W T G V O G D F U M G
                    P C G A Y H Q F L
                      O B D
```

Yet another successful operation!
You may now move on to Level 7.

Level 7

The IONizer

As you said earlier, Chi, a heroine's work is never done. The forces of evil are still afoot, and there is yet another mission to be completed. Remember those rogue prefixes that were wreaking havoc on correctly spelled words throughout the universe? We have just learned that there is a new group of rogue *suffixes* disguised as real suffixes causing problems all over the place. It seems that these suffixes are disguising themselves as the suffix **-ION**. Here's the problem, though. You see, the suffix **-ION** can be added to a *verb* (an action word) to change it to a *noun* (a person, place, thing, or idea). When the suffix **-ION** is added to a word such as ABBREVIATE, the suffix knocks off the silent **E** and takes its place. The new word is then: ABBREVIATION.

And that is exactly what should take place when **-ION** is added. But the rogue suffixes are holding on to that **E** when they attach themselves to the ends of the words. In other words, these mutants are changing these correctly spelled words into horrible shapes that we good guys can barely stand to look at!

What an outrage! Between rogue prefixes and rogue suffixes, innocent words are getting attacked from every direction!

Fortunately, Chi, we have a new weapon for situations just like this one. Our gadget experts have come up with a great new crime-fighting tool: the "IONizer." Here's how it works: Any time you see a word with **-ION** added to it incorrectly, use your IONizer to blast it into compliance. Don't worry, the effects of the IONizer won't harm the word, only the rogue suffix. Just so you don't go around blasting everything in sight with your new toy, we better take a look at some of the words that may have been affected by the rogue suffix attacks.

You nailed me! I'm starting to get an itchy trigger finger!

EQUATION	DESECRATION
SEPARATION	OBLIGATION
NARRATION	DECORATION
IRRITATION	GRADUATION
EVALUATION	INFILTRATION
CREATION	INSTITUTION
COORDINATION	GENERATION
ISOLATION	PARTICIPATION

Each one of the words in the list above was once a verb, just like our example (the verb ABBREVIATE) that we looked at earlier. The final **E** was replaced by **-ION** and then the new word, a noun, was ready to report for duty. The best part about this transformation is that none of the word parts were injured in the process. It is hoped that you can save many, many other words from the pain and agony that these rogue suffixes are inflicting.

Now, let's get down to the part we know you're dying to try out: the IONizer. But first, let's become a little more familiar with this particular group of words. You will now see a list of verbs that need to be transformed into nouns. Use your IONizer to add **-ION** to each of the following words. Remember: Our IONizer has special powers that will force a mutant suffix to let go of the **E**. That will allow you to write the new **-ION** word correctly in the blank next to each word. After you complete the IONizaton, check your work against the IONized list in the Appendix. Ready? Go to work! We have done the first one for you.

EQUATE	_EQUATION_	DESECRATE	_____
SEPARATE	_____	OBLIGATE	_____
NARRATE	_____	DECORATE	_____
IRRITATE	_____	GRADUATE	_____
EVALUATE	_____	INFILTRATE	_____
CREATE	_____	INSTITUTE	_____
COORDINATE	_____	GENERATE	_____
ISOLATE	_____	PARTICIPATE	_____

Great work! You're definitely getting the hang of that new gadget. The guys down in the weapons development center said it wouldn't take too long to master the IONizer. Let's do a little more work with these words before we actually have to use the IONizer in battle conditions. Take the rewritten words from above and put them in alphabetical order in the spaces below. Be careful to note the correct spelling of each one. When you finish alphabetizing, check the list against the list in the Appendix.

1. _____ 2. _____ 3. _____

4. _____ 5. _____ 6. _____

7. _____ 8. _____ 9. _____

10. _____ 11. _____ 12. _____

13. _____ 14. _____ 15. _____

16. _____

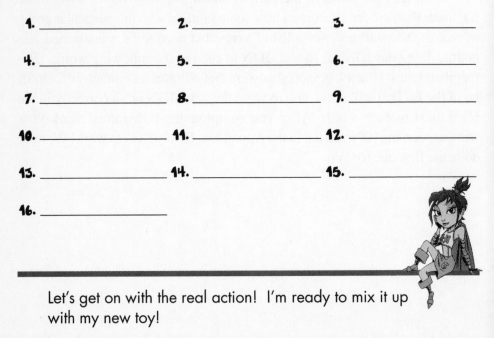

Let's get on with the real action! I'm ready to mix it up with my new toy!

Indeed you are, Chi! Before we throw you into the fray, however, let's go over the objective once more.

* Use your IONizer to undo any mayhem that the rogue suffixes have caused with unsuspecting words.

* Replace the silent **E** at the end of the word with **-ION.** *No other changes should be made.*

* DO NOT IONize correctly spelled words! We have no idea what may happen if you IONize a word that doesn't need to be IONized.

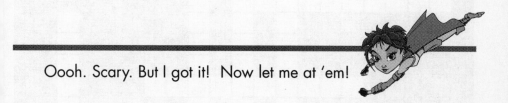

Oooh. Scary. But I got it! Now let me at 'em!

OK. Here's the plan. You have 16 words to check and see whether or not they have suffered at the hands of the rogue suffixes. If they have been affected, you will see a silent **E** being held in the clutches of a mad **-ION** suffix. Use your IONizer to break that hold and release the silent **E**. After IONization, place the word in the proper Debriefing Cells. If you find a word that doesn't need IONization, you should immediately place the word in the Debriefing Cells as well, so there is no chance that the rogue suffixes can affect it. You should check your results with the battle log in the Appendix. Be careful, and do a great job! Remember, the fate of who knows how many spellers is in your hands!

Level 7 Challenge

Complete the following puzzle challenge by correctly spelling the words on the next page and placing them in their corresponding boxes. Challenge solutions are in the Appendix.

DEBRIEFING CELLS

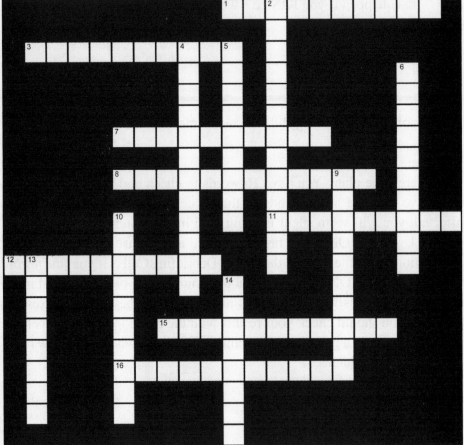

Get Wise! Mastering Spelling Skills

Across

1. SEPARATEION
3. IRRITATEION
7. EVALUATEION
8. COORDINATION
11. ISOLATEION
12. GENERATEION
15. DESECRATEION
16. INSTITUTEION

Down

2. PARTICIPATION
4. INFILTRATEION
5. NARRATEION
6. DECORATEION
9. OBLIGATEION
10. GRADUATION
13. EQUATEION
14. CREATEION

Outstanding! Once again the Word Warrior triumphs over the verbal vagabonds of the universe! You have successfully completed Level 7. You may advance to Level 8.

Level 8

Return of the Cloaking Device

Bad news, Chi. It seems that intelligence reports from earlier levels weren't complete. Somehow, a few of the same dastardly field agents who used the cloaking device in Level 5 escaped justice and unleashed the cloaking device on a second group of words! Just as in Level 5, the cloaking device shrouds and hides one of the consonants in a double-consonant set. This is especially serious because the list of words now targeted by the villains contains words that are often misspelled by students. You can save this list of words in the same way that you liberated the first list from the ill effects of the Double-Consonant Cloaking Device.

I heard you this time—*cloaking* device, not *choking* device!

Your experience with this type of verbal violation should be really invaluable in neutralizing the effects of the cloaking device. We have been able to gather several archived files of the affected words, and we have compiled a list for you below. Read through the words and become familiar with them. Keep in mind that the list below shows the words *before* the attack of the cloaking device.

AFFORD	**CORRESPONDENT**
IRRIGATION	**COLLAPSE**
AFFIRMATIVE	**ILLEGIBLE**
AFFECTION	**IRRESPONSIBLE**
SUFFICIENT	**OFFICIAL**
OFFERED	**AFFLICTION**
CORRUPT	**IRRESISTIBLE**
COLLISION	**ILLUMINATE**
ILLITERATE	

Do you have a solid picture of these words in your mind? Great. Because we will need to rely on superb mind-power skills in order to accomplish this heinous task! So, before we move on, in order to ensure you have these words firmly implanted in your brain, use your writing implement to go back through the list and underline the sets of double consonants. We've done the first one for you.

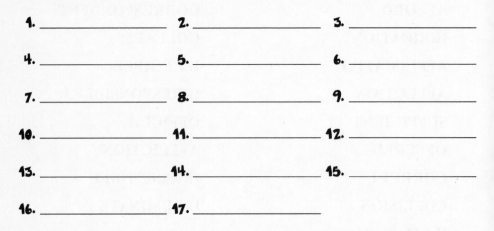

Double vision for double trouble in the galaxy!

You know, Chi, so many spellers are tempted to spell these words with a single consonant instead of double consonants that these were easy prey for the cloaking-device agents. That's what they do—target spellers' weaknesses and attack already difficult word groups. Fortunately for the spelling world, you can handle crises like these. It's almost time to get to work on the damaged words and restore them to their original preattack condition. Before you do, arrange the words from the list on page 45 into an alphabetical list. This will help you to remember and visualize the correctly spelled words. When you're done, compare your list with the one in the Appendix.

1. _____   2. _____   3. _____

4. _____   5. _____   6. _____

7. _____   8. _____   9. _____

10. _____   11. _____   12. _____

13. _____   14. _____   15. _____

16. _____   17. _____

Great work! You handled those like a pro. Now for the tough part. You saw the carnage from the first cloaking-device attack back in Level 5. However, it never gets any easier seeing maimed and disfigured vocabulary words. Those poor innocent words never knew what hit them. Hopefully you'll still have the stomach to deal with the carnage caused by the cloaking device. When you feel like your intestinal fortitude is such that you can stand to work with the mauled words, jump right in and start reconstructing the words. Use your writing implement to carefully place the reconstructed word in the blank next to the old, disfigured, and misspelled word. We do hope that this will be enough to save these words. To make sure you saved the words, compare your answers with those in the Appendix. We've done the first one for you.

Locked and loaded and ready for some action! Let me get to work!

AFORD	_AFFORD_	CORESPONDENT	_____
IRIGATION	_____	COLAPSE	_____
AFIRMATIVE	_____	ILEGIBLE	_____
AFECTION	_____	IRESPONSIBLE	_____
SUFICIENT	_____	OFICIAL	_____
OFERED	_____	AFLICTION	_____
CORUPT	_____	IRESISTIBLE	_____
COLISION	_____	ILUMINATE	_____
ILITERATE	_____		

It was easier to work on these words, but it doesn't get any easier to see these innocent words in their altered, mutated state!

Nice work, Chi, but unfortunately we have just received disturbing news from our safety inspectors. The cloaking device had an unusual effect on these words. Apparently, both letters in each of these double-consonant sets were damaged beyond what we originally had suspected. This means that our surgeons had to remove the entire double-consonant set from each word. It will be up to you to remember how each word is spelled and then *replace the double-consonant set*. Only by completing this delicate mission can you save these words and advance to Level 9. Prepare your writing implement and begin your operation. Be sure to check your work against the corrected list in the Appendix. The first one is done for you.

A <u>FF</u> ORD

I___IGATION

A___IRMATIVE

A___ECTION

SU___ICIENT

O___ERED

CO___UPT

CO___ISION

I___ITERATE

CO___ESPONDENT

CO___APSE

I___EGIBLE

I___ESPONSIBLE

O___ICIAL

A___LICTION

I___ESISTIBLE

I___UMINATE

Good steady hands and a delicate touch are sometimes just as important as brute strength.

You have successfully fulfilled your mission, and you may now advance to Level 9.

Level 9

The Dec*ie*vers

If you noticed that the title of Level 9 is misspelled, then you may have a pretty good idea of the problem we're facing here. We have just received a new report—not from our intelligence agents but from our historians. The historical department has been working closely with the intelligence agency to get to the bottom of an age-old mystery. You probably remember when you were much younger and first learning how to spell, there was a little jingle about **IE** and **EI** that made its rounds through every schoolhouse in the country. It went:

"**I** before **E** except after **C** . . ."

Seemed to be a good rule . . . didn't it? Well, our historians have done some serious research and have made an amazing discovery. Our intelligence agents have gone to great lengths to verify the historians' suspicions, and it is our job to break the news to you. Many, many years ago, even longer ago than we first suspected, the evil scholars began their work not in a deep-space lab but here on Earth! One of the first actions they took against spellers was the release of false information. The evil scholars are actually the ones who started that nasty, misleading misinformation.

Now that is low! I've been following that rule for years, and now I know why I still messed up so much!

Low indeed! How many millions of unsuspecting schoolchildren have been brainwashed by that age-old jingle? Who knows? Now that the truth is out, it is up to you to help eradicate this misinformation. We have issued a call for volunteer words to combat this misinformation campaign, and a number of words have shown up for service. It is your job to protect them and keep them safe. The first regiment of volunteers falls into the same category. Read through the list of volunteers. Can you see what they all have in common besides the fact that they are exceptions to the old "rule?"

NEIGHBOR	**WEIGHT**
SEINE	**THEIR**
FEIGN	**REINDEER**
FREIGHT	**VEIL**
HEINOUS	**NEIGH**
WEIGH	**REIGN**
REIN	**VEIN**
SLEIGH	

So, what do these words have in common? First of all, these words are living proof that the "**I** before **E** except after **C**" rule is bunk and bogus. Second, the **EI** combination in each of these words makes the long $\bar{a}$ sound like the **A** in LAKE or like the **I** in IN. We had such an overwhelming response to our call for volunteers that a second, smaller regiment has been assembled. Check out these new recruits:

FORFEIT	**SOVEREIGN**
SURFEIT	**FOREIGNER**
COUNTERFEIT	**FOREIGN**

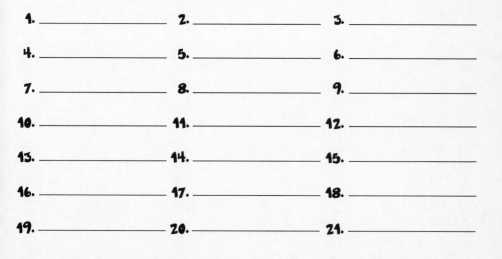

More of the bravest vocab in the universe!

Yes, Chi, they are putting duty and honor above personal safety. If the scholars were to find out that this group of words was combating the campaign of lies started in the evil lab here on Earth countless generations ago, they certainly would send agents to undermine your efforts. So that you are a little more familiar with your new recruits, let's put both lists into alphabetical order. Check your roster with the one in the Appendix.

1. _____   2. _____   3. _____

4. _____   5. _____   6. _____

7. _____   8. _____   9. _____

10. _____   11. _____   12. _____

13. _____   14. _____   15. _____

16. _____   17. _____   18. _____

19. _____   20. _____   21. _____

Outstanding organizational and spelling skills! However, while you were working, we received reports that the scholars are onto us. They have conjured up a horde of dec*ie*vers to attack and then replace the vocab volunteers. In order to combat this countereffort by the evil scholars, we have already deployed the volunteers. As we speak, they are engaged in hand-to-hand combat with the dec*ie*vers. They have engaged the enemy in an arena. We need you to go in and finish the job.

Here's the strategy: We have all the dec*ie*vers in one place but the volunteers are there, too. We need you to extract each of the volunteers one by one. Start with identifying the volunteers by using your writing implement to circle each volunteer. Next, extract each volunteer as you identify it and place the volunteer on a blank below the arena. It doesn't matter in which order you identify and extract the volunteers, as long as you extract all the volunteers and none of the dec*ie*vers. Can you handle it? Great! We knew you could! Just remember to verify your results with the log in the Appendix.

The Word Warrior is ready for the extraction process!

Level 9 Challenge

Complete the following puzzle challenge by identifying the 21 correctly spelled words. Challenge solutions are in the Appendix.

EXTRACTION ARENA

```
              M B P
          K Q M M F G U E H
        Y K I I T O M Z X F Y E H
      W B R S N Y R X H B E C Y E Y U Y
      C M I E E H I S X B C E L X U D J C H
    H O O Z E T E I F R O F R T R K T B N J L
    S N J U D G J D E U L N X R U U H F H C W
  J P F G G N U H C N V G G N O C B M Y G R I K
  B Q E G E E T L T N I E G H B O R H I B H Z Y
U P G W R I I M E E E W E I G H T W Y F K G S P K
U C I B H E R R E R T I A R L G K I E K D D I R V
W Q U X F N F M E G F J E S P I I Z S S U V E Z B
M H H M R R E R V V V V I S X B E Q C G J F K Y A U N
O B Q O X I I O L S F O R E I G N E R K D Z E B Q F J
F P F Y T E S U G I V V S B T N H C X K C X I D B F A
R F D H G U F P K S U P L H G V B F F V P E J V P
D E T T H R P H E R U D A I I A D S K F Z F Z I K
O Y I E T F K I F C S S E E E E B F M M Y M Z N Q
E X G O I N E H Z P L L R F G M F A K I K M K
N D I H E I N O U S X M S M U H H L H J G R Y
  I D I T E O H X E K W B H C T N X R R V D
  N V A Y V U F C V S P D W F I K R I R W F
    W Q K M S J M Y M S O T G M U V S L A
      K R C P P M G T H P L D V R V L C
        N T G G C X W C T E X R U
          K I U M D C Q E I
              P F Q
```

1. _____   2. _____   3. _____

4. _____   5. _____   6. _____

7. _____   8. _____   9. _____

10. _____   11. _____   12. _____

13. _____   14. _____   15. _____

16. _____   17. _____   18. _____

19. _____   20. _____   21. _____

**Congratulations on yet another outstanding mission!
You may now advance to Level 10.**

Level 10

Qryptonite

We have just made a startling discovery! Many, if not all, of the mutants released by the evil scholars have a weakness. Do you remember the weakness of the legendary superhero Superman? It was called "kryptonite," and it rendered the superhero virtually powerless. It was like Superman had some bizarre allergy to the kryptonite. According to our researchers, many of these mutants have their own kryptonite, and you won't believe what it is!

Let me guess. Is it pollen? honey? sugar? bee stings? chocolate? pet dander?

No, Chi, it's nothing like that at all. As it turns out, most of the mutant words from the evil laboratory are affected by the letter **Q** in the same way that Superman was affected by kryptonite. The letter **Q** makes these mutants writhe in agony and cause horrific pain. In a desperate act of self-preservation, some of the mutants have gone on a **Q**-snatching rampage. Clad in special **Q**-resistant outerwear, these mutants have kidnapped **Q**s from all sorts of spelling words. Cleverly, the mutants don't just leave the word wandering about without **Q**s. The mutants take the **Q**s *and* the **U**s that accompany the **Q**s. Remember that, unless you're spelling QATAR or IRAQ, a **Q** must always be followed by a **U**.

Those dumb mutants! Anybody could recognize words that are left without the **Q** and the **U**!

Not so dumb, Chi. The mutants replace the **QU** combination with two different letter sets in an attempt to confuse students everywhere. In words such as QUAKE, the mutants swipe the **QU** and replace that set with **KW**. The result of such a caper would be KWAKE, a word that sounds like the original but doesn't look like the original. Of course, the mutants hope no one will notice the difference.

The second example of the mutants' mayhem is what they are doing with words such as UNIQUE. In words where **QU** is pronounced like **CK**, the mutants replace the **QU** set with **CK**, hoping as before that no one will notice.

Even worse, the mutants are dumping all the **Q**s and **U**s in an interstellar garbage dump light years away. Miraculously, though, we rescued the letters and are debriefing them right now.

I bet the **Q**s and the **U**s are ready to be reunited with their old words!

Probably so, Chi, and that's exactly what we'll need you to do later. First, though, we need to get our list of **Q** words organized into two groups. Read through the list of words and take note of the words in which the **QU** combo sounds like **KW** and the words in which the **QU** combo sounds like **CK**. In the blank next to each word in the list, write **KW** or **CK** depending on how the **QU** sounds in the word. Two have been done for you.

UNIQUE	CK	**QUINTUPLET**	___
CLIQUE	___	**QUAINT**	___
PLAQUE	___	**QUENCH**	___
MASQUERADE	___	**BANQUET**	___
CONQUER	___	**ACQUAINTED**	___
LACQUER	___	**QUIZZICAL**	___
ACQUIRE	KW	**COLLOQUIAL**	___
ADEQUATELY	___	**QUIVER**	___
QUARANTINE	___	**INQUISITIVE**	___
SEQUEL	___	**QUESTIONNAIRE**	___

Excellent work! You definitely have the hang of the two **QU** sounds. Unfortunately, the mutants eliminated the **QU** from each of the words in the list.

Sadly, you will now find the aftermath of the mutants' attempts to rid the universe of **Q**s. Read through the next list, and use your trusty writing implement to rewrite each of the following words correctly in the blank next to each one. By rewriting these words correctly with your writing implement, it will be that much more difficult for the mutants to alter the words again later.

UNICKE	_____	KWINTUPLET	_____
CLICKE	_____	KWAINT	_____
PLACKE	_____	KWENCH	_____
MASCKERADE	_____	BANKWET	_____
CONCKER	_____	ACKWAINTED	_____
LACCKER	_____	KWIZZICAL	_____
ACKWIRE	_____	COLLOKWIAL	_____
ADEKWATELY	_____	KWIVER	_____
KWARANTINE	_____	INKWISITIVE	_____
SEKWEL	_____	KWESTIONNAIRE	_____

That writing implement is an amazing thing! There must be a hundred different things that the writing implement can do!

You can say that again, Chi. And you'll need it some more to battle with these mutants. Use your writing implement one more time to alphabetize the list of **QU** words. The mutants should stay away while you're working on your list. You can be rest assured, though, that they'll be back sooner or later, dressed in their **Q**-resistant suits, to replace the **QU**s with **CK**s and **KW**s again. Rewriting the words in alphabetical order will provide extra insurance against further mutant attacks. When you complete the organizational list, compare your work with the list in the Appendix.

1. _____ 2. _____ 3. _____

4. _____ 5. _____ 6. _____

7. _____ 8. _____ 9. _____

10. _____ 11. _____ 12. _____

13. _____ 14. _____ 15. _____

16. _____ 17. _____ 18. _____

19. _____ 20. _____

That ought to take care of those words! Double reinforcement against mutant attacks!

We wish we could tell you that the double reinforcement provided by your writing implement would be sufficient for the protection of the **QU** words. Unfortunately, we can't. In fact, the mutants may attack again sooner than we expected and with even stronger anti-**Q** suits than before. That means that the mutants might be able to get rid of the **Q**s again.

Therefore, we need to do two things: First, we need you to place each of the **Q** words inside a Mutant-Proof Forcefield until all the **Q**-proof mutant suits can be collected and destroyed. Second, we need to destroy the mutants' **Q**-proof suits; we'll take care of that. Quickly, now! We have no time to spare. We must conquer these mutants as soon as possible! The **Q** words each have a particular place within the forcefield to stay until the mutants have been eliminated. It will be up to you to figure out which **Q** word goes in each section of the Forcefield. We have given you a few clues, but the rest is up to you!

Level 10 Challenge

Complete the following puzzle challenge by filling in all the correctly spelled words from this level. Challenge solutions are in the Appendix.

MUTANT-PROOF FORCEFIELD

Great work, Chi! While you were busy sorting out the words and placing them inside the Forcefield, we lured all the mutants clad in **Q**-proof suits into a big room. We tricked them into leaving their **Q**-proof suits outside the room, and then we locked them inside. Imagine the look of horror on their faces when they saw the word QUARANTINE written a hundred thousand times on the walls of the room! It's safe to say that the hundred thousand **Q** words should be ADEQUATE to consider the mutants CONQUERED! I can hear their screams of pain from here!

Congratulations! You may advance to Level 11.

The Positronic Positive Identification Device

Despite all of your hard work thus far, the mutants are still working just as hard to confuse students. The latest development seems to be with some genetically altered mutant words. The evil scholars carefully selected a handful of words and cloned them. However, they made sure they altered the genetic makeup of the words. The result? Mutant words that both *look* and *sound* very much like the original word. All of the words in the group targeted by the genetic specialists contain either the letter **G** or **C**.

Here's the deal: The evil scholars had these words genetically engineered so the original words with **G** were reproduced with a **C** and vice versa. For example, the word TENACIOUS might look like TENAGIOUS, and the word DILIGENT might look like DILICENT. Some of these words might not be

too confusing, but some are kind of tricky if you aren't paying attention because some of the words actually *sound* like they *could* have either a **C** or a **G**
and still be correct!

**Leaping Lizards! It's just plain wrong to try and
confuse students like that! We won't even talk
about the ethics of cloning!**

Agreed, so let's get to work. Let's take a look at the original list of words that
the scholars cloned:

ELEGANT	**INNOCENCE**
APPLICANT	**NEGLIGENCE**
INTELLIGENT	**SIGNIFICANCE**
MAGNIFICENT	**EXTRAVAGANCE**
COMMUNICABLE	**OUTRAGEOUS**
ELIGIBLE	**SUSPICIOUS**
CONVINCIBLE	**CONTAGIOUS**
AMBIGUOUS	**CONSPICUOUS**

Gee, I see what you mean! Or should I say, *Cee*, I *gee* what
you mean!

Good eye, Chi. Now let's do a little exercise to help us become familiar with the correct spellings of these words. Use your writing implement to put the above list in alphabetical order. This will help reinforce the proper spelling in your mind's eye so that your final mission on this level will not be so difficult. Be sure to check your list with the one provided for your reference in the Appendix.

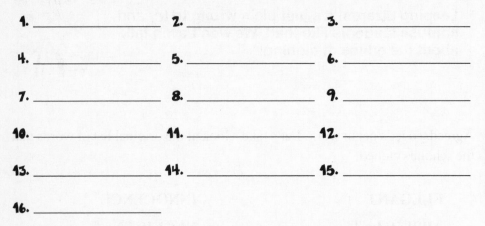

1. _____   2. _____   3. _____

4. _____   5. _____   6. _____

7. _____   8. _____   9. _____

10. _____   11. _____   12. _____

13. _____   14. _____   15. _____

16. _____

Excellent work! While you were hard at work, we managed to corral the mutants just long enough to get a digital image of them. Our computer geeks down in the digital lab have prepared a side-by-side comparison of the original words and the mutated clones. Read through the high-tech, digitally reproduced list of original and mutant words. As you read through the list, take this opportunity to try out your newest weapon in your arsenal: the Positronic Positive Identification Device, or Positron, for short. You can positively identify the original word by using your controls on the Positron. Set your controls so that the weapon can place a circle around the correctly spelled original word. Be sure to check your work against the Appendix. The first one has been done for you.

> **Sweet! The Positron! What a cool-sounding weapon! I wonder if it can help me positively ID what the heck our cafeteria serves on Fridays!**

(ELEGANT)

ELECANT

APPLIGANT

APPLICANT

INTELLICENT

INTELLIGENT

MAGNIFIGENT

MAGNIFICENT

COMMUNIGABLE

COMMUNICABLE

ELIGIBLE

ELICIBLE

CONVINCIBLE

CONVINGIBLE

AMBIGUOUS

AMBICUOUS

INNOCENCE

INNOGENCE

NEGLIGENCE

NEGLICENCE

SIGNIFIGANCE

SIGNIFICANCE

EXTRAVAGANCE

EXTRAVACANCE

OUTRACEOUS

OUTRAGEOUS

SUSPICIOUS

SUSPIGIOUS

CONTAGIOUS

CONTACIOUS

CONSPICUOUS

CONSPIGUOUS

That Positron is pretty outstanding, isn't it? We'll get plenty of use out of that Positron later on, so don't lose that thing! Now, back to the **C** and **G** mutants. You have reviewed the list of original words, and you've gotten a look at the mutants who are trying to masquerade as the originals.

OK, now this is where it is going to get dangerous. We need you to go deep into enemy territory where the original words are being held hostage. You will then have to identify the originals and distinguish between the originals and the mutants. Use your Positron to positively ID each original word and place a circle around each one. Only after your identification mission can our extraction team go in after the original **G** and **C** words from the previous page. For heaven's sake, though, please don't mistakenly identify any mutants because we can't have any extracted mutants running loose again! Only after you have extracted all the original words from the hostage area can the mutants be eradicated! Be careful, stay focused, and do a good job! Remember to check your work against the ID log in the Appendix.

Level 11 Challenge

Complete the following puzzle challenge by circling the 16 correctly spelled words. Challenge solutions are in the Appendix.

HOSTAGE AREA

```
C S S E B F                    U E O S S S
O R U I M P                    G Q I U U U
N T O O P R U                M Q S O O O O
T A I Z U T N                  A U U E E I I
A P G B C C Z M            K J G X C G C G
C P A I N T I Q                B I T N X A I I
I L T N M N R B N          G B R E S C R P P
O I N N E E C O M          M A C U O C T S S
U G O O C C O O T A      A V I O M O Z U U U
S A C G N I N U N Y      A L U M M F M O S S
  N J E E L V A A V R  C G C U M T A M A H
  T P N G L I C G W I A E I N U P G U I I E
    N C I E N T E A N N P I N F N G E X L
    B E L T G N L C V S C I C I K C L B Q
    M G N I A E C N A G I F I N G I S
    R E I B C K O B A R I B A T C R J
      N O L I C L B C C T C L I F I
      M D E L E L N E M I X L E N P
        I J P E G N W F O E E D W
        H A P L T T I C U L T L H
        G A I O N V O T E A W
        D L G G E I N R C C T
          E I V G N S A A C
          S B F I N P C N E
            L Y F O I E T
            E J I C G O X
            Z N E U U
            A G N O S
              A C U
              M E S
```

Congratulations on another successful mission!
You may now advance to Level 12.

Level 12

The Forgotten Letters

We're dealing with something very evil on this level—more so than just some mutants wandering around snatching letters or masquerading as innocent words. What we're dealing with is a force so great, so powerful, so ancient that only one person, or maybe two, in the entire universe is capable of dealing with such a menace.

That would be me! Hey, who's the other great one?

The force that must be reckoned with here dates back perhaps even further than your English teacher's birth certificate. The mysterious force of Level 12 will mess with your mind, and you'll never even know it happened. The force we have to face here is one that makes students completely forget about certain letters of the alphabet! Our historians, our researchers, and our intelligence agents have not been able to discover the source of the force, but we're pretty sure it also came from that dark laboratory run by the evil scholars. We have, however, discovered two things that will help keep the effects of this force to a minimum.

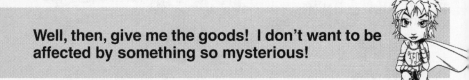

Well, then, give me the goods! I don't want to be affected by something so mysterious!

The first thing we have learned that can help protect you from this mysterious force is aluminum foil. Now, follow these instructions carefully:

1. Stop reading this book immediately, go to the kitchen, and find the aluminum foil.

2. Tear off several large pieces of the foil.

3. Wrap one or two pieces around your head like a helmet.

4. Wrap one piece around each of your forearms and then stick a few pieces between your toes.

We're serious. Put the book down and do this immediately! This is based on good intelligence!

Uh ... This is getting kind of scary, and I'm having serious doubts regarding the sanity of the author . . .

I know this sounds bizarre, but you *must* trust me. Now, the second thing that will protect you against this force is practicing with the words that the force exploits. We have obtained an archived list of words the force exploits by altering students' minds. Perhaps you're wondering what effect this force has. Read the list and see if you can figure out what effect the force has had on students and may continue to have on students for generations and generations to come:

SOPHOMORE	WHISTLE
COMFORTABLE	KITCHEN
POSTPONE	BUDGET
QUANTITY	HANDSOME
ETCETERA	RECOGNIZE
ENVIRONMENT	GOVERNMENT
GOVERNOR	FEBRUARY
WEDNESDAY	ELEMENTARY
JEWELRY	ENTERTAINMENT

Did you notice anything unusual about the words? Read them again, but this time say them out loud. Did you notice anything that time? Now if you were wearing the foil as we instructed, you would have noticed that each of the words in this list is pronounced as if one of the letters in the word *isn't there*. Did you pick up on that? If not, you really should go wrap yourself in foil as we suggested!

I felt silly at first, but now the shiny, metallic look is kind of growing on me.

Read through the list again. This time, as you read through the list, use your writing implement to rewrite the word in the blank next to the word. Then, use your writing implement to underline the letter or letters in each word that aren't pronounced when the word is spoken. The first one has been done for you.

SOPHOMORE	SOPH<u>O</u>MORE	WHISTLE	_____
COMFORTABLE	_____	KITCHEN	_____
POSTPONE	_____	BUDGET	_____
QUANTITY	_____	HANDSOME	_____
ET CETERA	_____	RECOGNIZE	_____
ENVIRONMENT	_____	GOVERNMENT	_____
GOVERNOR	_____	FEBRUARY	_____
WEDNESDAY	_____	ELEMENTARY	_____
JEWELRY	_____	ENTERTAINMENT	_____

Nice work! See what a difference the foil makes? It's kind of like using garlic to keep vampires away—it works. For whatever reason, when these words are spoken, at least one of the letters stays silent. That doesn't mean that the letters aren't important, though. They still have to be included in the words in order for the words to be spelled correctly. Despite what the force may make the unprotected mind believe, every letter is special and important. Why so many students have been vulnerable to the effects of this force is unclear, but we've finally figured out how to fight the force.

With guns that shoot aluminum-foil bullets?

Not exactly, Chi. What we'll need to do is . . . you guessed it . . . sort them into alphabetical order first. Then, we'll have to put the words into a specially designed Holding Cell for a while. We'll get to that in a few minutes. Alphabetize the words and be extra sure that they are spelled exactly right. Every time the words are spelled the way they were *designed to be spelled*, the force is weakened. Be sure to check your list against the list in the Appendix.

Anything to weaken the force, man! Writing implement ready!

1. _____ 2. _____ 3. _____

4. _____ 5. _____ 6. _____

7. _____ 8. _____ 9. _____

10. _____ 11. _____ 12. _____

13. _____ 14. _____ 15. _____

16. _____ 17. _____ 18. _____

Excellent alphabetizing skills! You're getting really good at this! Now that the force has been weakened, you have one final task to perform that should put the proverbial nail in the coffin for the mysterious force that makes students forget the letters in these words.

Look at the misspelled words in the list below and then rewrite them correctly in the special Holding Cells. Be sure to spell the words exactly right. The Holding Cells will continually emanate the very essence of these words outward into the farthest reaches of the universe. That should go a long way toward destroying the mysterious force unleashed by the evil scholars. It is very important that you do this correctly, but we have complete faith in you. Do a great job, and then check your work against the Appendix.

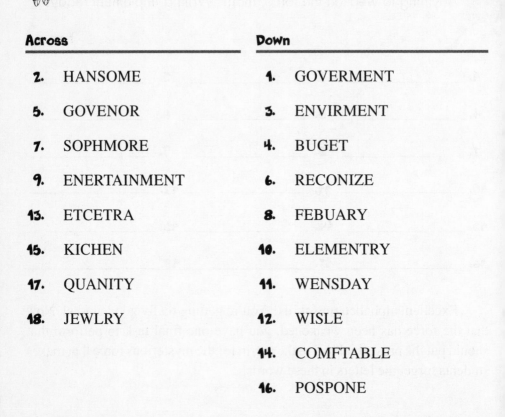

The Word Warrior versus the Mysterious Force— sounds kind of like a movie, doesn't it?

Across

2. HANSOME
5. GOVENOR
7. SOPHMORE
9. ENERTAINMENT
13. ETCETRA
15. KICHEN
17. QUANITY
18. JEWLRY

Down

1. GOVERMENT
3. ENVIRMENT
4. BUGET
6. RECONIZE
8. FEBUARY
10. ELEMENTRY
11. WENSDAY
12. WISLE
14. COMFTABLE
16. POSPONE

Level 12 Challenge

Complete the following puzzle challenge before advancing to the next level. Challenge solutions are in the Appendix.

HOLDING CELLS

Congratulations! You have successfully foiled the force and may now advance to Level 13.

Level 13

The E-Plenisher

We just received a rather disturbing report from intelligence agents in the field. Do you remember the E-Zapper that you used on the first few levels to eliminate the Es that didn't belong in words? Well, we suffered a security breach, and one of our E-Zappers was stolen. Our guess is that the mutants from the scholars' evil lab took the E-Zapper, but we're not sure. The bottom line is this: The E-Zapper, one of the most powerful verbal weapons in the universe, has been turned against the forces of good and is now being used to further the cause of evil.

We have learned that the E-Zapper has already been used against a group of unsuspecting words, and so their fate is now in your hands. Let's take a look at the list of words that has been assaulted by the villains who stole the E-Zapper. Keep in mind that this is an archived list that shows the words in their original state before the E-Zapper assault.

The nerve of those guys! Using our own weapons against us! That's just wrong!

MERELY	**SENSELESS**
LONELY	**PRICELESS**
TIMELY	**ENGAGEMENT**
LOVELY	**STATEMENT**
SINCERELY	**AMUSEMENT**
LIKELY	**CONFINEMENT**
IMMEDIATELY	**MEASUREMENT**
SEVERELY	**ADVERTISEMENT**
COMPLETELY	**INTENSELY**
DEFINITELY	

As you read through this list, you've probably figured out why the mutants used the E-Zapper against these words. These words all include a silent **E** that easily could be forgotten or left out by spellers. By E-Zapping that silent **E**, the mutants figured they could dupe spellers everywhere and trick them into permanently leaving out the silent **E**. As you surely already know, the effects of the E-Zapper are more or less permanent, so our backs are against the wall here. Fortunately, our weapons experts have been working overtime to develop a weapon to combat the effects of the E-Zapper. While they continue their efforts in the weapons lab, let's take a look at the digital image of the affected words we managed to capture after the E-Zapper attack. As you read through the list, use your writing implement to rewrite each word correctly in the blank next to it. After you rewrite the words, check your work against the list in the Appendix.

MERLY	_____	SENSLESS	_____
LONLY	_____	PRICLESS	_____
TIMLY	_____	ENGAGMENT	_____
LOVLY	_____	STATMENT	_____
SINCERLY	_____	AMUSMENT	_____
LIKLY	_____	CONFINMENT	_____
IMMEDIATLY	_____	MEASURMENT	_____
SEVERLY	_____	ADVERTISMENT	_____
COMPLETLY	_____	INTENSLY	_____
DEFINITLY	_____		

It's always so sad to see these words like this, just a shell of their former selves!

It's sad indeed, Chi. However, just in the nick of time, our weapons guys have developed a brand new, state-of-the-art weapon to combat the effects of the stolen E-Zapper. The new weapon is called the E-Plenisher. The E-Plenisher blasts an **E** back into a word that has been E-Zapped! Don't worry, the words won't feel a thing. This new weapon is top secret, and the mutants have no idea that we have this weapon. We'll use the element of surprise to mount effective resistance to the effects of the E-Zapper. Before we try out our new weapon, let's familiarize ourselves a little more with the words that were affected by the E-Zapper's powerful rays. Put the words into alphabetical order and make sure you check your list against the alphabetized file in the Appendix.

1. _____   2. _____   3. _____

4. _____   5. _____   6. _____

7. _____   8. _____   9. _____

10. _____   11. _____   12. _____

13. _____   14. _____   15. _____

16. _____   17. _____   18. _____

19. _____

Great work! Now we're ready for the E-Plenisher! Here's how it works: You'll see the list of affected words below with a few spaces in each word. Use your E-Plenisher to replenish the missing **E** in each word. Be sure to focus the E-Plenisher on the correct part of the word so that the **E** is placed in the correct space. Just like the effects of the E-Zapper, the effects of the E-Plenisher are irreversible. As always, be sure to check your final results against the Appendix. The first one has already been done for you.

Great! No pressure!

MER_E_L__Y   SEN__S__LESS

LON__L__Y   PRIC__L__ESS

TIM__L__Y   ENGA__G__MENT

LOV__L__Y   STAT__M__ENT

SINCER__L__Y   AMU__S__MENT

LIK__L__Y   CONFIN__M__ENT

IMMEDIAT__L__Y   MEASUR__M__ENT

SEVE__R__LY   ADVERTIS__M__ENT

COMPLE__T__LY   INTENS__L__Y

DEFINIT__L__Y

Eureka! The E-Plenisher works, and you were masterful in its use! Thankfully, the words have been returned to their original state and a good portion of the words is out of danger once again ... at least for now. Be sure you have your Positron fully charged because you may need it again very soon.

Congratulations! You have successfully completed Level 13 and may now advance to Level 14.

Level 14

The Masquerading Mutant Marauders

The mutants are up to their old tricks again. In earlier levels you were faced with the task of identifying mutant words that had assumed the identities of real words. We are hoping that experience will come in handy because you are going to be battling those same mutants once again. The sad fact is that the mutant words continue to attack innocent words causing all sorts of problems. But … the particular mutants you will be facing in *this* level are especially crafty because they chose a rather random assortment of words to imitate.

Mutants! Those hideous creatures! They are the reason I get up in the mornings! Someone has to make the universe safe for spellers!

And it's a good thing, because you do a great job! Now, let's take a look at the words the mutants are copycatting. Read through the list carefully and take special note of the correct spelling of each word. Also, make sure your Positron is fully charged!

RECESSION	PROFESSION
PROCESSION	UNNECESSARY
CONCESSION	UNCONSCIOUS
CONSTITUTION	PRONOUNCE
PERSUADE	MISSPELL
DISSUADE	PARALLEL
INTERMISSION	PERSEVERANCE
PROPORTION	PERFORATED
DISSATISFIED	PERENNIAL
PERMISSION	SUBCOMMITTEE

The Word Warrior sees a pattern here! These are all tricky words!

You're right, Chi. Your verbal powers are obviously far greater than those of the guys in our research department. They detected nothing. These words don't have much in common except that they can all be pretty tricky for spellers. Of course, the other thing they have in common is the fact that they've all been copycatted by the evil mutants. Undoubtedly, the scholars cloned these particular words because they thought the mutants could go relatively unnoticed, especially by young or inexperienced spellers. That's why you have been called in for this mission.

Is your Positron ready for action? Good! We'll be using that shortly. Read through the list again, but this time use your writing implement to underline the potentially tricky part or parts of each word. The first one has been done for you.

I am the Wizard of the Writing Implement!

RE<u>C</u>ESSION	PROFESSION
PROCESSION	UNNECESSARY
CONCESSION	UNCONSCIOUS
CONSTITUTION	PRONOUNCE
PERSUADE	MISSPELL
DISSUADE	PARALLEL
INTERMISSION	PERSEVERANCE
PROPORTION	PERFORATED
DISSATISFIED	PERENNIAL
PERMISSION	SUBCOMMITTEE

Nice use of the writing implement! As you certainly noticed, the scholars knew what they were doing when they picked these words for mutation because each one has a part that can be treacherous. Before you actually go into battle, though, you should do a little more prep work. This is going to be an especially challenging mission so you can't be overprepared.

Therefore, we need you now to organize the list above into an alphabetical list so that the correct spelling of each word is reinforced in your mind. You'll need your exceptional brainpower for this mission. Be sure to verify your alphabetized list with the one provided in the Appendix.

1. _____ 2. _____ 3. _____

4. _____ 5. _____ 6. _____

7. _____ 8. _____ 9. _____

10. _____ 11. _____ 12. _____

13. _____ 14. _____ 15. _____

16. _____ 17. _____ 18. _____

19. _____ 20. _____

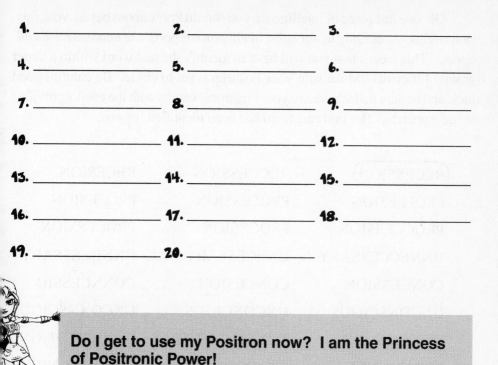

Do I get to use my Positron now? I am the Princess of Positronic Power!

We're almost there, Chi! Outstanding work with the alphabetizing! Now you're ready to be briefed on the mission. The mutants have gone a step further than just imitating the words from the list. Somehow, the mutants have captured the words and have hidden them far away in a prison camp for correctly spelled words!

Your job is to infiltrate the camp and identify the correctly spelled, real words with your Positron. All mutant words will then be eradicated by our special forces. That means it is imperative that the real words be identified correctly. Get in and get out quickly! And don't let the Positron fall into enemy hands . . . We all remember what happened when the mutants got a hold of one our E-Zappers!

Oh, one last piece of intelligence you should know about before your mission begins. According to our latest intelligence reports, *the mutants have multiplied*. This means that you will have to identify the real word within a larger group of mutants. Make sure your Positron is set to circle. Be careful, good luck, and be sure that you verify your Positronic results with the results provided in the Appendix. The first real word has been identified for you.

(RECESSION)	RECCESSION	RECESION
PROFFESION	PROFESSION	PROFESION
PROCCESSION	PROCESION	PROCESSION
UNNECCESSARY	UNECESSARY	UNNECESSARY
CONCESSION	CONCESION	CONNCESSION
UNCONSCIOUS	UNCONCIOUS	UNCONNSCIOUS
CONSTITUON	CONSTUTUTION	CONSTITUTION
PORNOUNCE	PRONOUNCE	PRONNOUNCE
PROSUADE	PURSUADE	PERSUADE
MISSPELL	MISPELL	MISPPELL
DISSUADE	DISUADE	DISSUDE
PARALLEL	PARRALLEL	PARRALEL
INTROMISSION	INTRAMISSION	INTERMISSION
PERSERVERANCE	PERSEVERANCE	PRESEVERANCE
PROPORTION	PORPORTION	PURPORTION
PERFORATED	PORFORATED	PERFERATED
DISSATISFIED	DISATISFIED	DISSATIFIED
PERRENIAL	PERRENNIAL	PERENNIAL
PERMISION	PERMISSIN	PERMISSION
SUBCOMITEE	SUBCOMMITEE	SUBCOMMITTEE

That was some of the trickiest Positronic work we've ever witnessed. Great work! The words have been identified and are being rescued as we speak. Within minutes the mutants will be destroyed, never to confuse students again!

A masterful mission! You may now advance to Level 15.

Level 15

Hostel Mutant *Hoard* Engages *Inn Fowl* Play

My intelligence has just unveiled an*other* disturbing piece of information sure to affect spellers everywhere. Two evil scholars from that dark, horrible laboratory have created three top-secret groups of special-operation mutants, one of which is known as the Mutant *Hoard* (we'll battle the other special-operations mutants on a different level). The Mutant *Hoard* is a tenacious regiment of mutants who prey on spellers' weaknesses with homophones.

Homophones are words that sound alike but are spelled differently and have different meanings. For example, the words HORDE and HOARD are homophones. They sound exactly alike, but HORDE means "a large group" while HOARD means "a stockpile." Therefore, just by calling these special-op mutants the "Mutant *Hoard*," the evil scholars are well on their way to inciting chaos in the minds of spellers in our galaxy and beyond!

They'll have to get up pretty early in the morning to fool Chi! Hmm ... that sounds so much weirder when I say it than when my grandparents do!

Here's how this special-op force works: Basically, the members of the Mutant *Hoard* can sneak into any written material—textbooks, dictionaries, novels, comic books ... you name it—and search for words that are homophones.

When the *Hoard* finds a homophone, they take the word into custody and replace the word with its homophone, a member of the Mutant *Hoard*, in order to confuse and bewilder. Their hope is that students will just accept what is written as correct. Then, when the students becomes a speller, he or she will inadvertently misspell all the homophones.

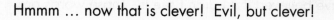

Hmmm ... now that is clever! Evil, but clever!

You should now take a look at the list of homophones that are the targets of the Mutant *Hoard*. Just so there's no confusion, we've provided not only the list of homophones but also the meanings of each homophone just so you can keep everything organized in that data storage unit between your ears. As you read the list, look for each word's homophone and how each sounds alike but is spelled differently.

PRINCIPLE—rule

CAPITAL—center; money

HORDE—large group

STATIONARY—still, motionless

VILE—evil

DESCENT—downward movement

FOWL—bird

HOARD—stockpile

DISSENT—differ

PRINCIPAL—main, central

REVIEW—look over

CAPITOL—important building

VIAL—bottle or container

COMPLIMENT—praise

HOSTEL—boardinghouse

REVUE—theater production

ISLE—island

HOSTILE—belligerent

AISLE—passageway

FOUL—offensive

STATIONERY—paper for correspondence

COMPLEMENT—balance, harmonize

I wouldn't have believed it if I didn't see it! Those words are confusing!

Only at first, Chi. Once you become familiar with them, you won't have any problems spelling them or identifying them. You probably noticed that each pair of homophones is pronounced almost exactly the same way. You probably also picked up that each pair of homophones was spelled similarly. It's the meanings of these homophones that distinguish them from one another. Therefore, to master this level, you will need to develop a mastery of the spellings as well as the meanings of these words. That's nothing the Word Warrior can't handle. To begin your preparations for battle, look at the list of words on page 91. In the column of blanks next to each word, write in the correct homophone. Be sure to check your list against the Appendix. We've done the first one for you.

Get Wise! Mastering Spelling Skills

AISLE   <u>ISLE</u>

CAPITAL

COMPLEMENT

DESCENT

FOUL

HOARD

HOSTEL

PRINCIPAL

REVIEW

STATIONARY

VIAL

These guys kind of look alike, too!

They sure do, Chi. That's why it takes a Word Warrior to handle the Mutant *Hoard* and the trickery the mutants use to confuse students. Now that you're starting to get a handle on the spellings of these homophones, let's become a little more familiar with the meanings of these homophones. Now you'll see the meanings for each of the homophones. In the blank next to each definition, use your writing implement to correctly spell the word that matches the definition. The first one has been done for you.

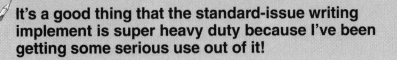

It's a good thing that the standard-issue writing implement is super heavy duty because I've been getting some serious use out of it!

large group	_horde_	paper for correspondence	_____
center; money	_____	still, motionless	_____
evil	_____	main, central	_____
differ	_____	bottle or container	_____
praise	_____	passageway	_____
island	_____	boardinghouse	_____
bird	_____	theater production	_____
look over	_____	offensive	_____
rule	_____	important building	_____
belligerent	_____	balance, harmonize	_____
stockpile	_____	downward movement	_____

Great work! Now you have proven that you're ready for battle against the Mutant *Hoard*! You'll need your Positron for this mission. Our reading specialists have extracted several complete sentences, some of which have been attacked and infected by the Mutant *Hoard*. These complete sentences have been corralled for your observation. Carefully work through each of the following sentences with your Positron locked and loaded. As you encounter the homophone in each sentence, carefully examine it. If the homophone is spelled correctly and, therefore used properly in the sentence, use your Positron to circle and identify it. If the sentence contains a mutant, use your writing implement to alter the mutant. In other words, if you suspect that the word is infected, change it to its proper spelling. When you have completed your mission, our Mutant Eliminators will take all sentences not marked with a Positronic circle to Sublevel 23 for purging. Be sure to double-check your work with the Appendix. Understand your mission? Excellent! Go get 'em!

Those mutants are gonna be sorry they ever messed with me! Just wait until they get purged from these sentences!

1. The travelers sought refuge in the small ~~hostile~~ *hostel* just off the highway.

2. The hunters observed dozens of species of foul, but they never saw the elusive dodo bird.

3. The bride tripped as she walked down the aisle; the groom knew he would get in trouble later, but he laughed out loud anyway!

4. The clever car salesman knew that the way to get big sales was to dish out big complements.

5. The stationary bike is the most boring exercise machine in the gym, besides the treadmill, the rowing machine, the stair-master, and the ab machine.

6. The vial little man never sends birthday cards to his family.

7. Our drama department's spring revue was absolutely spectacular!

8. The principle gave me lunch detention for six weeks for putting worms in her spaghetti.

---

9. There's no need to hoard the peanuts; my little brother already sucked all the chocolate off of them anyway!

10. The winning candidate was shocked to learn that the loser rolled the capitol with toilet paper after the election results were finalized.

11. As he started his dissent down the stairs, he tripped over his shoelace, tumbled down the stairs, and became the laughingstock of the school.

Outstanding work! The Mutant Eliminators are purging the remaining sentences right now, and the Mutant *Hoard* can be considered wiped out! The Mutant *Hoard*, thanks to your delicate Positronic work, will never harass those homophones again and will never bother readers and students again!

Congratulations on completing Level 15!
Advance carefully to Level 16!

Level 16

The MegaGlue 2000

OK, so it turns out that all our high-tech gadgetry and top-secret weaponry won't do you a bit of good now because the mutants have resorted to a rather old-fashioned form of mayhem. They have now targeted words that are composed of a root word and a suffix. To wreak havoc on these words, the mutants planted small explosive devices inside each word and blew them apart, leaving the words in pieces. That means that your job is somewhat primitive but no less important than the heroic tasks you have already performed on our other levels. Your mission is simple: Find the roots *and* their suffixes and glue them back together again. But you will need to use our handy glue-dispensing device, the MegaGlue 2000.

Sounds like we're in a pretty *sticky* situation!

You can say that again, Chi! But we've collected some important data on those poor, wounded words. Although quite a few words were attacked at different times and in different places, we've organized them into groups with some striking similarities. Let's take a look at the first group of targeted words as they appeared *before* they were detonated:

DEPENDABLE	**DEPENDANCE**
ACCEPTABLE	**ACCEPTANCE**
APPEARANCE	**IGNORANCE**
OBTAINABLE	**ALLIANCE**
APPROACHABLE	**COMPLIANCE**
DETECTABLE	**RESEMBLANCE**
CLEARANCE	**ATTENDANCE**

Did you notice a pattern or any similarities between most of the words in this list? Obviously each of these words consists of a root and a suffix. However, most of these words also contains a root that can stand alone as a word. For example, DEPENDABLE is made up of the root DEPEND + the suffix -ABLE. But, as a result of the demolition crew attacks, the word DEPENDABLE has been blown apart and is now separated into its root and its suffix. That poor, blown-apart word *now* looks like this: DEPEND ABLE.

A few of these words are composed of roots that need the final **Y** or silent **E** dropped when the suffix is added. Did you notice them? We're talking about IGNORANCE, ALLIANCE, COMPLIANCE, and RESEMBLANCE. So, when *they* were blown apart, the roots were left without the **Y** or **E** so they don't look exactly the way they normally would. Did you notice that each of these words also ended in either **-ABLE** or **-ANCE**? That's the other thing these words have in common.

Those demolition mutants knew exactly what they were doing, blowing those words apart like that! They may be primitive, but they're still *pretty* clever!

Let's take a look at the second group of words as they appeared before the mutant demolition. As you read through the list, look for similarities among words in this group:

COMPATIBLE	SUPERINTENDENT
SUSCEPTIBLE	INDEPENDENCE
PERMISSIBLE	CONFIDENT
IMPOSSIBLE	PERMANENT
INCREDIBLE	CONFIDENCE
EXPERIENCE	ADJACENT
INGREDIENT	PROMINENT

These all end in -IBLE, -ENCE, or -ENT. Thanks to my astute powers of observation, nothing gets by me!

So, there you have it: These two lists of words contain all the words that the demolition crew has demolished. In order to get ready to pick up *all* the pieces and put them back together again with your MegaGlue 2000, combine the lists and put the entire group of words into alphabetical order.

Put all the pieces together again? Why don't we just call all the King's horses and all the King's men?

1. _____

2. _____

3. _____

4. _____

5. _____

6. _____

7. _____

8. _____

9. _____

10. _____

11. _____

12. _____

13. _____

14. _____

15. _____

16. _____

17. _____

18. _____

19. _____

20. _____

21. _____

22. _____

23. _____

24. _____

25. _____

26. _____

27. _____

28. _____

Great work! You're just about ready to start working with your MegaGlue 2000. What you'll see on the following page is, quite frankly, a big jumbled mess. But we've rounded up the roots and suffixes that were blown apart. Your job is to find the root and the suffix that go together, apply a liberal amount of MegaGlue with your MegaGlue 2000, and make sure the root and suffix stick together. Suffixes are on page 100. Be sure to double-check your work with the Appendix!

ROOTS

COMPAT	_____	SUPERINTEND	_____
CLEAR	_____	ATTEND	_____
SUSCEPT	_____	INDEPEND	_____
DETECT	_____	RESEMBL	_____
PERMISS	_____	CONFID	_____
APPROACH	_____	COMPLI	_____
IMPOSS	_____	PERMAN	_____
OBTAIN	_____	ALLI	_____
INCRED	_____	CONFID	_____
APPEAR	_____	IGNOR	_____
EXPERI	_____	ADJAC	_____
DEPEND	_____	DEPEND	_____
INGREDI	_____	PROMIN	_____
ACCEPT	_____	ACCEPT	_____

SUFFIXES

-ENT	-ANCE	-IBLE
-IBLE	-ABLE	-ENT
-ENT	-ENCE	-IBLE
-ANCE	-ANCE	-ENCE
-ENT	-ANCE	-ABLE
-ABLE	-ENT	-ABLE
-ANCE	-IBLE	-ENT
-ENCE	-ABLE	-IBLE
-ANCE	-ANCE	-ANCE
-ANCE		

Uh, I kind of got some of the MegaGlue on my finger and then I scratched my nose. Now my finger is stuck, and from the side it looks like I'm picking my nose. Help!

Outstanding work, as always! You handled the MegaGlue 2000 like a pro. Hopefully, after the glue sets and dries, the words will be fixed permanently. We'll have to get our intelligence agents on the trail of the demolition crew or else they will turn up again on another level!

Congratulations! You have successfully completed Level 16 and may now advance to Level 17.

Level 17

The Dec*ie*vers, Part 2

Remember those brave vocab volunteers from Level 9 who answered the call to fight the misinformation of the evil scholars' "**I** before **E** except after **C**" rule? Well, we've issued another call for vocab volunteers, and yet again the brave words have answered our call. It seems that more dec*ie*vers have been located by our intelligence agents and our spy satellites throughout the universe. At this very moment, the new recruits are luring the dec*ie*vers into a trap so that we can eliminate them once and for all. In order to distinguish the real vocab words from the dec*ie*vers, you should familiarize yourself with the archived list of volunteer **EI** words.

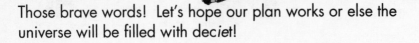

Those brave words! Let's hope our plan works or else the universe will be filled with dec*iet*!

RECEIVE	NEITHER
RECEIPT	PROTEIN
CEILING	SEIZURE
CONCEIVE	WEIRD
CONCEITED	HEIGHT
DECEIVE	LEISURE
DECEIT	CAFFEINE
PERCEIVE	FAHRENHEIT
SEIZE	INVEIGLE
EITHER	

There you have it! Those are the words that have joined forces with the Word Warrior to take on the dec*ie*vers. Those malicious mutants want nothing more than the total and utter confusion that would result from bewildered spellers. That's why you must prevail over the forces of evil! To better familiarize yourself with the list of recruits, organize the list into an alphabetical roster. Be sure to check your roster with the one provided in the Appendix.

With me as their fearless leader, these words can overcome anything that the evil scholars can muster up! Chi the Verbal Vixen can vanquish any vile, verbal … uh, I can't think of anymore V words. Oh well.

1. _____ 2. _____ 3. _____

4. _____ 5. _____ 6. _____

7. _____ 8. _____ 9. _____

10. _____ 11. _____ 12. _____

13. _____ 14. _____ 15. _____

16. _____ 17. _____ 18. _____

19. _____

Excellent work! Now you need to take the next step toward fighting and defeating the evil dec*ie*vers. The volunteers have almost all the dec*ie*vers in one place. While we wait for the signal from the volunteers to go in and eliminate the dec*ie*vers, you have one more training exercise to complete. Fire up your Positron and locate the correctly spelled word in each of the following pairs of words. Set your Positron to circle. Also, be sure to check your work with the Positronic results in the Appendix.

RECEIVE/RECIEVE   NIETHER/NEITHER

RECIEPT/RECEIPT   PROTEIN/PROTIEN

CEILING/CIELING   SIEZURE/SEIZURE

CONCIEVE/CONCEIVE   WEIRD/WIERD

CONCIETED/CONCEITED   HEIGHT/HIEGHT

DECEIVE/DECIEVE   LEISURE/LIESURE

DECIET/DECEIT   CAFFIENE/CAFFEINE

PERCEIVE/PERCIEVE   FAHRENHEIT/FAHRENHIET

SEIZE/SIEZE   INVEIGLE/INVIEGLE

IETHER/EITHER

You finished your Positronic work just in the nick of time! The volunteers have cornered all the dec*ie*vers in a spaceship. Your job is to go into the ship, Positronically identify our volunteers, and then get out safely; our extraction team will follow and extract the good guys. After we have extracted all the volunteers, the spaceship will be blasted into the outer reaches of the universe where the mutants will be sucked into a black hole never to bother spellers again. So use your Positron to identify the volunteers listed on page 106. Be very careful not to accidentally identify any of the mutants, or we could end up extracting a mutant and rocketing a volunteer into the depths of space. Ready for action? Great! Get in, get out, and stay safe!

The Positronic Princess is down with blasting off mutants! Let's go!

Level 17 Challenge

Complete the following puzzle challenge by identifying The Good Guys, which are listed on the following page. Challenge solutions are in the Appendix.

SHIP OF DEC*IE*VERS

```
      J W A I J X C F
      B H H T I L R M K
      N E G T V L I K N O
      M Y Z S X E U E P B G
      S E K P H M I Z S V X
      I T U Z T N U G U V B
      F P P S H P R T P X R Z
      G V R E C I E V E I C E D
      B L R O I E H R R S X P K G A P C Z O T J U
R       H P D I T C T Q C T B J F D Y W B E I V I K O
X S T W E G N Y E E N I E F F A C T E V E I C N O C A
G D J U O B G H R I R E Z I S H T O R H N O L V E   L N
G E S X D F F Y U N N V E U V R V E N O N K S I X     Q T
G I B P X C F V Z Z W E I R D E T E I C N O C E N S D R H F
M     V G L J Z I I R P S L L N R D E C E I T G I G R B G A
      Z K L W D E U M T A K D H U I N V E I G L E Z P L I W
T     Q Q A S R S Q M X P Q A I V A I L B D T E V I E C E D
K P R J Y N D I A V C A F F I E N E I T O R P E R U U S H
R F W O H C E W A I J C V Y G T C N R G Y H V S D L S
H O D G U L J C C G K J O H I E G H T H R Q I S Y U
A X T J Y I N F D D U I O V R A
M     S O P L I P L B E E U M
      D H D N A E G H C Z F W
      I H F E C Q Z K E B J
      H B J W L E S I Y Q C
      Y Z E V Z K S M V E
      T F Y H F A F D Q Y
      A M S F J W W H K
      B I U K Q C I J F
      B J S J F S L A
```

THE GOOD GUYS

RECEIVE
RECEIPT
CEILING
CONCEIVE
CONCEITED
DECEIVE
DECEIT
PERCEIVE
SEIZE
EITHER

NEITHER
PROTEIN
SEIZURE
WEIRD
HEIGHT
LEISURE
CAFFEINE
FAHRENHEIT
INVEIGLE

Outstanding Positronic work! The correctly identified volunteers have been extracted safely and the spaceship is ready for blast-off! Launch sequence activated … 3 … 2 … 1 … See you later, mutants!

You have successfully completed Level 17 and may now advance to Level 18.

Level 18

The Double Double Clones

Several levels earlier you battled the effects of the Double-Consonant Cloaking Device. As you may recall, the cloaking device was designed by the evil scholars to hide one consonant in a double-consonant set so that students would spell double-consonant words incorrectly. Well, we have a new problem … except the problem is reversed. The evil scholars created double double clones and released them into the universe. The double double clones were mutated from words containing double-consonant sets.

Double double clones … mutants so nice they named them twice! Not!

However, the mutation of each of the double double clones is an extra double-consonant set within the word. In other words, the double double clones have an extra set of double consonants within the word.

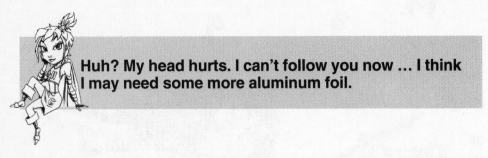

Huh? My head hurts. I can't follow you now ... I think I may need some more aluminum foil.

No, Chi. Too much aluminum foil is not good for anyone. Now pay attention; it's not so hard.

OK, I'm ready and focused!

For example, the double double clone of AGGRESSIVE might look like this: AGGRESSIVVE.

That's so horrible! I could barely look at that word, all hurt and mutated like that. Is it in pain?

I'm afraid so. The evil scholars thought they could really throw us for a loop with a double attack, one attack from the Double-Consonant Cloaking Device and one attack from the double double clones.

Let's examine the list of the double-consonant words targeted by the mutant double double clones. Keep in mind that these words are in their original, unaltered state. As you read through the list, use your trusty writing implement to underline the double-consonant set (or sets) in each word. Of course, we've done the first one for you.

CO<u>RR</u>OBORATE	AGGRESSIVE
IMMACULATE	ACCLAIM
MAYONNAISE	ACCOMMODATE
AGGRAVATE	RACCOON
CONNOISSEUR	ACCORDION
STACCATO	AGGRIEVED
ACCUMULATE	ACCOMPLISH
ACCOST	

Nice work! That writing implement just keeps going and going, doesn't it? Judging from the list, the evil scholars were on the right track. Just think of all the students out there who might be affected by the evil mutants. Your success in this mission is as imperative as any mission you have undertaken up to this point. So that you have the images of the correctly spelled words planted firmly in your mind, organize the list above into alphabetical order. As always, be sure to double-check your work with the alphabetized list in the Appendix. Keep using that writing implement; it is super heavy duty and should last for years to come.

I've done such amazing work with my writing implement that they're going to retire the number 2!

1. _____ 2. _____ 3. _____

4. _____ 5. _____ 6. _____

7. _____ 8. _____ 9. _____

10. _____ 11. _____ 12. _____

13. _____ 14. _____ 15. _____

Terrific! The words have been organized correctly, and we're ready for one more training exercise before you face the final challenge of this level. On page 111, you will see the list of words with blanks in each word. Each word should contain only one double-consonant set. Use your writing implement to double only *one* consonant in each word. Obviously, one blank in each word will have a letter in it and one blank will remain, well, blank. Use your writing implement wisely and verify your results with the key in the Appendix!

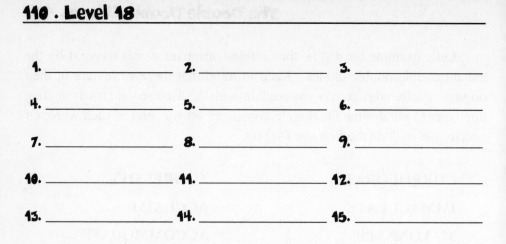

You know, the Appendix in this book is a lot more valuable than the appendix that my cousin had removed in surgery!

Get Wise! Mastering Spelling Skills

COR__OB__ORATE   AG__R__ESSIVE

I__MAC__ULATE   AC__L__AIM

MAYON__AIS__E   AC__OMMOD__ATE

AG__RAV__ATE   R__AC__OON

CON__OISSEUR__   AC__ORD__ION

STAC__AT__O   AG__RIEV__ED

AC__M__ULATE   AC__OM__PLISH

AC__OS__T

Your training is now complete and you're ready for your mission. Your mission, should you choose to accept it, is to identify the correctly spelled words from the list on page 113 and place them in the Safe House. Once the original words have been placed in the Safe House, our agents will take care of the double double clones. You don't want to know what happens to those mutants! Read each word of each word pair very carefully, then place the correctly spelled words into the appropriate place in the Safe House. Do a good job. Remember that millions of students are counting on you!

Level 18 Challenge

Complete the following puzzle challenge by choosing the correctly spelled words from page 113 and placing them in the Safe House. Challenge solutions are in the Appendix.

THE SAFE HOUSE

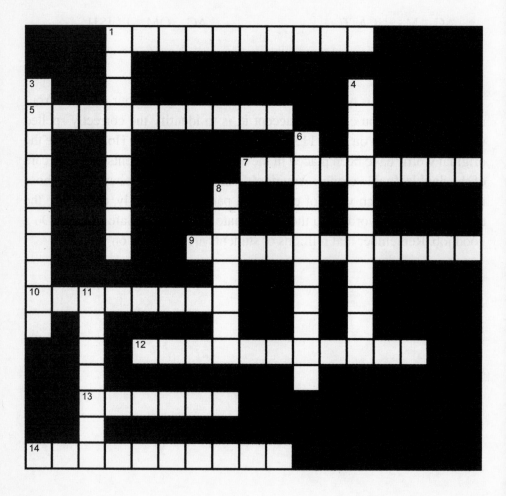

Get Wise! Mastering Spelling Skills

Across

1. ACCUMULATE/
   ACCUMMULATE

5. AGGRESSIVE/
   AGGRRESSIVE

7. ACCORDION/
   ACCORDDION

9. ACCOMMODATE/
   ACCOMMODDATE

10. STACCATTO/STACCATO

12. CONNOISSEUR/
    CONNOISSEURR

13. ACCOST/ACCOSST

14. IMMACCULATE/
    IMMACULATE

Down

1. AGGRIEVVED/
   AGGRIEVED

3. MAYONNAISE/
   MAYONNAISSE

4. CORROBORATE/
   CORROBBORATE

6. ACCOMPLISH/
   ACCOMMPLISH

8. RACCOON/RRACCOON

11. ACCLLAIM/ACCLAIM

Very nicely done! The mutants are now off to meet their fate and the real words are being debriefed in the Safe House. You have done students everywhere a great service by your work here! The evil scholars should take notice— the Word Warrior will prevail!

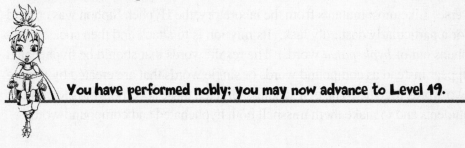

You have performed nobly; you may now advance to Level 19.

Level 19

The Hyphen Siphon

Our intelligence agents have just reported one of the more unusual, if not just plain bizarre, stories we've ever encountered. It looks as though the evil scholars in their vile laboratory have created a strange, mutantlike parasite known as the "Hyphen Siphon." This genetically engineered beast is just another rotten piece of the puzzle in the evil scholars' plan to foul up spelling across the universe. Like most mutants from the laboratory, the Hyphen Siphon was created for a particularly dastardly task. Its mission is to attack and then suck the hyphens out of *hyphenated* words. The result: words that should be hyphenated appear instead as compound words or single words that are created by joining two words together. The evil scholars targeted these specific words to confuse students and to make them misspell both hyphenated and compound words.

114

The ultimate goal of the evil scholars was to use the Hyphen Siphon to suck the universe dry of all its hyphens. In a universe void of hyphens, students would forever be confused about which words are hyphenated and which words are not.

Those sorry suckers! They must be stopped! We'll have to find that parasite and eliminate it ASAP!

You can say that again! Before we try to track down the Hyphen Siphon, let's take a look at some words that it might attack. All the words below should be hyphenated as shown:

LONG-TERM   **SISTER-IN-LAW**

RIGHT-HANDED   **LEFT-HANDED**

All fractions written as words should be hyphenated and all compound numbers should be hyphenated. Look at the examples below:

TWO-THIRDS   **THREE-FIFTHS**

TWENTY-THREE   **SEVENTY-ONE**

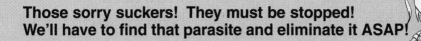

Well, what about the words that students might think should be hyphenated but really aren't?

Good question, Chi. Those are called "compound words," and below you will find a list of some pretty commonly misspelled compound words. You may think these guys have been sucked dry by the Hyphen Siphon, but they are *just the way they should be*:

BACKGROUND	PLAYGROUND
ELSEWHERE	NOWHERE
NEWSSTAND	NEWSROOM
ROOMMATE	TEAMMATE
PLAYWRIGHT	COPYRIGHT
WHOEVER	BOOKKEEPER
GRANDMOTHER	GRANDPARENT
NEARSIGHTED	FARSIGHTED

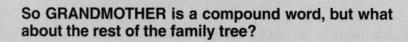

So GRANDMOTHER is a compound word, but what about the rest of the family tree?

Good question, Chi. All the *in-laws*, like SISTER-IN-LAW in the first list, are hyphenated. The other relatives like GRANDFATHERS, GRANDKIDS, and so on, are compound words without hyphens. Here's the only tricky part (and wouldn't the Hyphen Siphon love to get its grubby lips on this): GREAT-GRANDPARENTS, GREAT-UNCLE, and so on, are hyphenated between GREAT and whatever comes next. The GRAND part of the word still has no hyphen.

If the Hyphen Siphon attacked a family tree, would that make it a termite?

Where do you come up with these things, Chi! Let's get focused and ready for the challenge of defeating the Hyphen Siphon. Let's get these guys organized alphabetically. Being the Word Warrior that you are, you probably already knew this, but alphabetizing hyphenated and compound words is no different from alphabetizing any other words. Start with the first letter of the word, go to the second if necessary, and so on. If by some chance you have to sort beyond the hyphen, just move right past the hyphen without giving it a second thought. Ready to organize these guys? Good. Use the twenty-four words from the three lists along with GREAT-GRANDPARENTS and GREAT-UNCLE. When you finish the alphabetizing, double-check your list with the one in the Appendix.

1. _____
2. _____
3. _____
4. _____
5. _____
6. _____
7. _____
8. _____
9. _____

10. _____
11. _____
12. _____
13. _____
14. _____
15. _____
16. _____
17. _____
18. _____

19. _____
20. _____
21. _____
22. _____
23. _____
24. _____
25. _____
26. _____

Excellent work! Now you'll need to use your Positron to identify the correctly spelled words. Don't worry. The misspelled words are just holographic images that we're going to use for training purposes. While you're training, our mutant elimination team will be working on luring the Hyphen Siphon into range so they can take the sucker out! Set the Positron for circling, train hard, and be sure to verify your training results with the log in the Appendix! The first one has been done for you.

I train so I can inflict pain ... only on the Hyphen Siphon and other mutants, of course!

(TWO-THIRDS)   THREEFIFTHS

TWOTHIRDS   THREE-FIFTHS

TWENTYTHREE   SEVENTYONE

TWENTY-THREE   SEVENTY-ONE

BACKGROUND   PLAY-GROUND

BACK-GROUND   PLAYGROUND

ELSEWHERE   NO-WHERE

ELSE-WHERE   NOWHERE

NEWS-STAND	NEWS-ROOM
NEWSSTAND	NEWSROOM
ROOM-MATE	TEAMMATE
ROOMMATE	TEAM-MATE
PLAYWRIGHT	COPYRIGHT
PLAY-WRIGHT	COPY-RIGHT
WHO-EVER	BOOKKEEPER
WHOEVER	BOOK-KEEPER
GRAND-MOTHER	GRAND-PARENT
GRANDMOTHER	GRANDPARENT
LONG-TERM	SISTER-IN-LAW
LONGTERM	SISTERINLAW
NEAR-SIGHTED	FARSIGHTED
NEARSIGHTED	FAR-SIGHTED
RIGHTHANDED	LEFTHANDED
RIGHT-HANDED	LEFT-HANDED

You performed well in your training exercise, and it's a good thing, too. Our mutant elimination team totally underestimated the cunning of the Hyphen Siphon. The Hyphen Siphon attacked a large group of words, carried them back to its Lair, and then sucked the hyphens right out of them. Strangely, though, the Hyphen Siphon also dragged a number of compound words into its Lair. Apparently it didn't have time to sort them all out before it started sucking. Therefore, 23 words are trapped in the Hyphen Siphon's Lair.

Your job is to extract the words. After extraction, place them in one of two columns. The column on the left is for compound words that do *not* need to be rehyphenated. The column on the right is for words that have been stripped of their hyphens and need to undergo rehyphenization therapy. As you place these words in the column on the right, be sure to include a hyphen in the proper location so that the rehyphenization therapists can do a thorough job. You've probably noticed that some of the words are words you have dealt with earlier in this level and some are not. Handle the unfamiliar words as you would the ones you saw earlier in this level. Place the hyphen between the distinct, or individual, words in the compound word. You'll see. You can handle it! Before you allow the rehyphenization therapists to begin their work, check your columns with those in the Appendix. Ready for extraction? Go get 'em and bring 'em back alive!

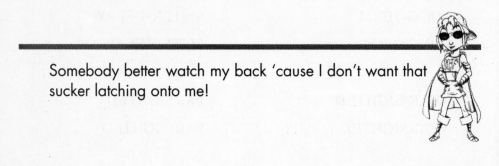

Somebody better watch my back 'cause I don't want that sucker latching onto me!

Get Wise! Mastering Spelling Skills

Level 19 Challenge

Complete the following puzzle challenge by removing the words from the Lair and putting them in the appropriate column on page 122. Challenge solutions are in the Appendix.

THE LAIR OF THE HYPHEN SIPHON

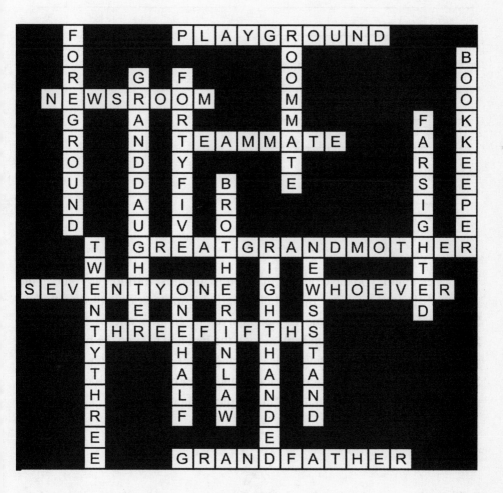

<u>**Without Hyphens**</u>　　　　　　　　　　<u>**With Hyphens**</u>

_____　　　　_____

_____　　　　_____

_____　　　　_____

_____　　　　_____

_____　　　　_____

_____　　　　_____

_____　　　　_____

_____

_____

_____

_____

_____

_____

    Once again, you have proven that you're the most formidable force in the universe! By the way, our mutant elimination team took care of the Hyphen Siphon. They planted some C-4 explosives in another one of the Hyphen Siphon's Lairs. The Hyphen Siphon took the bait and sucked the hyphen right out of the C-4. Being a very volatile substance, the C-4, or C4 after the Hyphen Siphon sucked out the hyphen, exploded and nobody has been able to find any piece of the Hyphen Siphon larger than a piece of confetti.

Talk about going out with a bang!　　　　**You may now advance to Level 20.**

Level 20

Return of the Rogue Prefixes

One of the first levels you mastered was one in which rogue prefixes attacked innocent prefixes and assumed their identities. Our field agents have just informed us that a number of new, meaner, and *nastier* rogue prefixes are on the loose.

These new mutants have mutated even more than the first rogue prefixes you defeated. According to our intelligence, this new breed of mutants works in groups. A group of these mutants typically swarms around a group of innocent words and assumes the identities of the prefixes. Then, the prefixes detach themselves from the words and switch words with the other rogue prefixes. As a result, a group of words that formerly was spelled correctly will end up in a big jumbled mess. For example, if the evil mutant prefixes ambushed the words ANTISEPTIC and INTRAMURAL, the prefixes would do their dirty deeds on the words and the result would be as follows:

*INTRA*SEPTIC and *ANTI*MURAL

Wow! That is a mess! Those darn mutants!

Yes, Chi, those darn mutants, as you put it, are at it again. They attacked several smaller groups of words at various times and have really made a mess for spellers. It's going to be up to the Word Warrior to sort things out. While our field agents try to round up all the affected words, let's take a look at an archived digital image of the affected words in their original, unaltered state:

TRANSLUCENT	**PERMEATE**
INTERVIEW	**HYPOTHESIS**
ANTECEDENT	**TRANSCONTINENTAL**
SUPERFICIAL	**HYPERACTIVE**
ANTISEPTIC	**CIRCUMSCRIBE**
PERSPIRE	**SUPERINTENDENT**
INTRAMURAL	**INTERCOLLEGIATE**
CIRCUMNAVIGATE	**INTRAVENOUS**

What about SUPERHERO?

Our field agents have located nearly all of the affected words, and they are en route to a staging area where it is hoped you can straighten out these guys and get the spellings corrected permanently. All indications are that the words will

Get Wise! Mastering Spelling Skills

be salvageable once the mutant prefixes are replaced with new mutant-proof prefixes. We'll get to that later, though. Right now, we need to get this list organized and sorted. Use your handy-dandy writing implement and organize these words into alphabetical order so that you have a handy-dandy reference tool for when you have to reconstruct these words. Use the handy-dandy Appendix to check your list after you finish.

Enough with the handy-dandy stuff already!

1. _____   2. _____   3. _____

4. _____   5. _____   6. _____

7. _____   8. _____   9. _____

10. _____   11. _____   12. _____

13. _____   14. _____   15. _____

16. _____

The field agents have the words, mutant prefixes and all, corralled at the staging area. It will be imperative that you recognize the mutated words, and that you are able to reconstruct the words correctly. Perhaps a training exercise to get you ready for battle is what you need. On your final mission, as well as any other time that you might need to spell these words on your own, you will need to be able to spell these words correctly. That begins with recognizing and correcting misspelled words such as the ones in the following training area. The words in the training area below are all jumbled up. Use your writing implement to mark through the prefix for each mutated word and write the correct prefix above the old one. The first one has been done for you.

Doesn't it seem like the Word Warrior is always cleaning up someone else's mess?

TRANS
~~INTER~~LUCENT

INTERTHESIS

PERCEDENT

INTRAFICIAL

TRANSSEPTIC

SUPERSPIRE

CIRCUMMURAL

HYPERNAVIGATE

ANTEMEATE

HYPOVIEW

ANTICONTINENTAL

CIRCUMACTIVE

INTRASCRIBE

PERINTENDENT

TRANSCOLLEGIATE

SUPERVENOUS

Now those were some messed-up words! Nothing I couldn't handle, but messed up nonetheless!

What a difference the right prefix makes, huh? Those were definitely some messed-up words, and that's exactly what they looked like until just a few minutes ago. Apparently, Chi, your reputation precedes you. When the mutants heard that you were training, they turned tail and ran. That's right. The mutants took off like they just stole something, and we haven't seen nor heard from them since. However, even though the mutants are out of sight, they aren't out of mind. They left quite a mess behind when they skedaddled. Basically, we have a bunch of words that are missing their prefixes and a bunch of new prefixes that need to be added to the words. Take out your writing implement and set it to act as a Prefix Affixer. Match up the new prefix and the word to which it should be attached, and then make the fix. Place the newly reconstructed words on the blanks below so they have time to bond. Be careful to affix the correct prefix to each word; we can't have permanently bonded misspelled words. Check your final results against those in the Appendix. The first one has been done for you.

NAVIGATE	CEDENT
LUCENT	INTENDENT
SCRIBE	SEPTIC
CONTINENTAL	ACTIVE
VIEW	FICIAL
THESIS	VENOUS
COLLEGIATE	SPIRE
MEATE	MURAL

PREFIXES

TRANS-	SUPER-	TRANS-	SUPER-	HYPER-
INTER-	HYPO-	PER-	ANTE-	CIRCUM-
PER-	INTRA-	CIRCUM-	INTER-	INTRA-	ANTI-

CIRCUMNAVIGATE _____   _____

_____   _____

_____   _____

_____   _____

_____   _____

_____   _____

_____   _____

Those words look so much different when they are put together correctly. You obviously did a great job fixing what the mutants messed up. Thanks to you, the students of the universe are free to spell safely and correctly again, but only temporarily.

You have done well, and you may now advance to Level 21.

Level 21

The Evil Mind of Dr. Diablo

You aren't going to believe what our intelligence agents dug up this time! Here's the latest intelligence from our guys undercover. Deep within the evil scholars' laboratory is a wing called the "Biological Warfare Wing." In that dreaded wing works a mysterious biologist named Dr. Diablo. When Dr. Diablo was in junior high, he participated in a local spelling bee. He did quite well until the final round when he had to spell the word PARALLEL. He spelled it:

P-A-R-A-L-E-L

Diablo was devastated and humiliated. As a result, he turned to a life of crime, devoted to making spellers and students screw up as often as possible. Because he misspelled PARALLEL by forgetting an **L**, Dr. Diablo feels deep-seated hatred for all words with a double-L set. But rather than create a mutant, Dr. Diablo created the L Diablo virus, a virus that attacks words like PARALLEL and causes the word to lose one of its **L**s. Intelligence reports indicate that this virus has been released into the atmosphere and a number of words have been infected. We have put together a composite of the words that have been infected by the virus. Read through the list carefully:

Should I wear some kind of mask or something? Maybe gloves? Do we have any cans of disinfectant lying around somewhere?

OSCILLATE	ALLURE
ALLOTMENT	ALLUDE
COLLABORATE	COLLUSION
PARALLEL	ALLEGIANCE
SATELLITE	METALLIC
MISCELLANEOUS	SKILLFUL
BALLOON	VILLAIN
ELLIPSE	COLLISION

Are you starting to get a glimpse into the evil mind of Dr. Diablo? These innocent **LL** words probably had no idea what hit them when they were infected. Nevertheless, they have been infected, and only the Word Warrior can save them. Before you actually start dealing with the victims of the virus, you need to become more familiar with the words you'll be trying to save. Arrange the list in alphabetical order. This will help you in your training, and it will give you a point of reference for when you actually encounter the virus victims. Be sure to double-check your work with that in the Appendix.

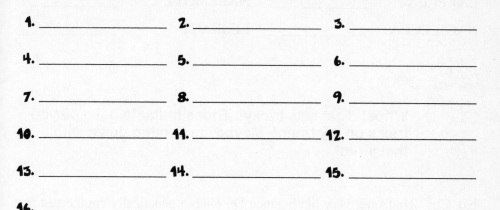

1. _____   2. _____   3. _____

4. _____   5. _____   6. _____

7. _____   8. _____   9. _____

10. _____   11. _____   12. _____

13. _____   14. _____   15. _____

16. _____

Outstanding work! This list will be vital to you once you start working closely with the infected words. We need you to complete one more training exercise before we send you into the quarantined area with the words that have been compromised by the L Diablo virus. Look at the following list of words and you will see that the letters have been jumbled. Each jumbled word, though, contains only one **L** instead of the usual double-**L** set. In the blank next to each word, use your writing implement to reconstruct the word with the proper double-**L** set. Try to do a good job here, but realize that this is only a training mission. There is no pressure here. The fate of the words is not totally dependent on your performance at this point. Just breathe deeply, focus, and try to reconstruct the words as best you can. The first one has been done for you.

COILISON	COLLISION	LISTETAE	_____
ALUER	_____	COLUISON	_____
NABOOL	_____	COSTILAE	_____
VINAIL	_____	UDEAL	_____
BREATOLOAC	_____	SPELIE	_____
FISKLUL	_____	SICALENEMOUS	_____

LARPELA   _____   NALEMOTT   _____

NAGILECEA   _____   LIMEACT   _____

Whoa! That was tricky! Those mutants have played tricks on my brain! Maybe I'm coming down with that virus!

No, Chi. That's not very likely since Dr. Diablo genetically engineered that virus to only attack words with a double-**L** set. Maybe you should be worried if *Chi* is really short for *Chinchilla* but not otherwise. During your training exercises, our biohazard team rounded up and quarantined all the infected words. In order for the words to be able to fight off the L Diablo virus, they must all be placed in the Antiviral Disinfectant Area. You'll see the list of infected words below, with the **L** missing from each. Take each word and carefully place it into the Antiviral Disinfectant Area. Be careful, though, because the words will only fit when they are spelled correctly. Make sure you get them placed properly and securely so they can be disinfected. Use the clues in the Antiviral Disinfectant Area for where to place the words. Ready? Do a great job!

OSCILATE	ALURE
ALOTMENT	ALUDE
COLABORATE	COLUSION
PARALEL	ALEGIANCE
SATELITE	METALIC
MISCELANEOUS	SKILFUL
BALOON	VILAIN
ELIPSE	COLISION

Level 21 Challenge

Complete the following puzzle challenge by correctly spelling the words on page 132 and placing them in the Disinfectant Area. Challenge solutions are in the Appendix.

ANTIVIRAL DISINFECTANT AREA

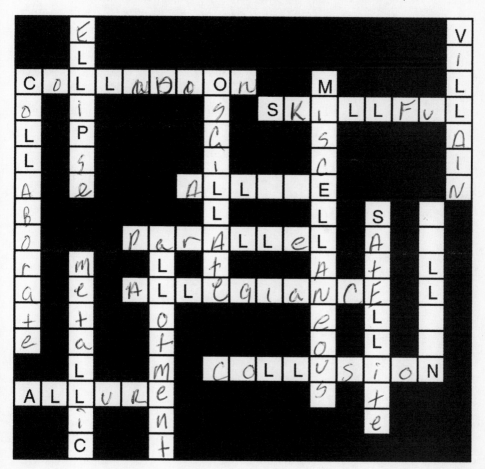

You did it! A little longer in the Antiviral Disinfectant Area and these words will be as good as new! As for Dr. Diablo, we'll send in a sweeper team and deal with him as soon as we find the lab.

Nice virus vanquishing! You may now advance to Level 22.

Level 22

Only K Can Save the Day

As you almost certainly know, there are many words out there that contain the letter **C**. In some words the letter **C** has a soft sound, more like an **S** sound, and is considered a "soft **C**," like in the words:

CITY, ICY, and CERTAINLY

On the other hand, there are words like:

COUNT and CAMERA

In these words, the letter **C** has a hard sound, more like a **K** sound, and is considered a "hard **C**." For most students, these differences are usually pretty easy to figure out. However, the evil scholars have found a weak link in the system. They believe they have found a way to confuse these students.

Those nefarious, nasty, naughty scholars! They just can't leave well enough alone, can they!

Here's where the evil scholars plan to do their dastardly doings. Take a look at the list of words below and you'll notice that they are all words that end in the letter **C**, a hard **C**:

PANIC	STATIC
FROLIC	PICNIC
COLIC	TRAFFIC
POLITIC	MIMIC
SHELLAC	ZINC

When a student wants to add **-ED**, **-Y**, or **-ING** to these words, they can't just slap those suffixes onto the words. After all, just try pronouncing PANICED with a soft **C** or STATICY with a soft **C**; it just isn't the same. In order to prevent this, the letter **K** must be added to the word so that PANICED becomes PANICKED, and so on. This is what the evil scholars want everyone to forget. Therefore, in an effort to mess with everyone's minds, the scholars have released a number of mutant words into the universe to cause problems. Here is a list of the words that have been mutated. Take careful notice of the placement of the **K** in each word so that the **C** can stay hard.

They won't mess with the Word Warrior's mind, especially if I keep wearing all that aluminum foil from several levels earlier.

PANICKY	TRAFFICKED
PANICKED	TRAFFICKER
PANICKING	TRAFFICKING
PICNICKED	MIMICKED
PICNICKER	MIMICKING
PICNICKING	COLICKY
FROLICKED	POLITICKING
FROLICKER	SHELLACKED
FROLICKING	ZINCKY
STATICKY	

Try pronouncing those words without the letter **K**!
That would sound pretty crazy!

You can say that again, Chi! Thankfully we have that letter at our disposal so we don't have a bunch of really crazy-sounding **C** words. However, there are some out there, and they're mutants! And, we'll need you to once again save the day, you and **K**, that is. We can't stress enough how important it is for you to get those mutants out of circulation, so to speak. Our researchers are working around the clock trying to figure out exactly how to deal with these mutants once we locate them and isolate them. While they are working out the details, let's become a little more familiar with the words that have been mutated. Take the list from above and alphabetize them in the blanks on page 138. Make sure you double-check the Appendix for the correct order. If at any point your writing implement begins to get dull, energize it immediately so that your work will stay sharp!

1. _____ 2. _____ 3. _____

4. _____ 5. _____ 6. _____

7. _____ 8. _____ 9. _____

10. _____ 11. _____ 12. _____

13. _____ 14. _____ 15. _____

16. _____ 17. _____ 18. _____

19. _____

Looks like the writing implement is working just fine! Nice work! Before you actually go to work with the mutants, let's do a little practice so that your skills are in tip-top shape for the actual mission. Below is a digital image of the words plus a suffix. You need to attach the suffixes to the words by adding a **K**. After all, that's the glue that makes the suffixes stick! Double-check your work with the completed words in the Appendix. The first one has been done for you.

PANIC + Y	PANICKY	TRAFFIC + ED	_____
PANIC + ED	_____	TRAFFIC + ER	_____
PANIC + ING	_____	TRAFFIC + ING	_____
PICNIC + ED	_____	MIMIC + ED	_____
PICNIC + ER	_____	MIMIC + ING	_____
PICNIC + ING	_____	COLIC + Y	_____
FROLIC + ED	_____	POLITIC + ING	_____
FROLIC + ER	_____	SHELLAC + ED	_____
FROLIC + ING	_____	ZINC + Y	_____
STATIC + Y	_____		

Now you're ready for action! The researchers have discovered that the mutants are unusually docile and harmless. Apparently the evil scholars messed up! Because these mutants are harmless, our research lab has come up with a pretty clever way to deal with these mutants. Instead of eliminating them, your job will be to place them carefully into a pool of liquefied vitamin K. Believe it or not, when these mutants come in contact with vitamin K, a **K** suddenly appears in the correct place in the word. Prolonged contact with vitamin K makes the change permanent. You'll see the words + suffixes below. Just place them in their numbered positions in the vitamin K pool on page 140 and *voilá!* Do a great job! Be sure to check the pool in the Appendix to make sure the changes are correct and permanent!

Across

2. PICNIC + ING
4. MIMIC + ING
7. PICNIC + ER
8. FROLIC + ER
9. STATIC + Y
11. PANIC + Y
13. POLITIC + ING
14. TRAFFIC + ING
15. SHELLAC + ED
16. FROLIC + ED

Down

1. MIMIC + ED
3. ZINC + Y
5. TRAFFIC + ER
6. COLIC + Y
7. PANIC + ING
8. FROLIC + ING
10. TRAFFIC + ED
11. PANIC + ED
12. PICNIC + ED

Pool? Should I get my floaties and my sunscreen?

Level 22 Challenge

Complete the following puzzle challenge by adding a **K** to each word from page 139 and placing correctly in the pool below. Challenge solutions are in the Appendix.

LIQUEFIED VITAMIN K POOL

Get Wise! Mastering Spelling Skills

Excellent! Those words are soaking up every drop of vitamin K. Very soon, the mutants won't be mutants anymore!

Congratulations! You have successfully completed Level 22, and you may now advance to Level 23.

The Pluralizer

Now that you have advanced all the way to Level 23, we feel you are ready for one of the trickiest hordes of mutants ever released into the universe by the evil scholars: the Horde of Misspelled Plurals!

These mutants have nothing in common except that they are mutations of normal, plural words. We're sure you know that most words can be made plural by simply adding **S**, as in MUTANTS, WARRIORS, or SCHOLARS. Other words, however, need a little more than just **S**. To form the plural of words ending in **S**, **SS**, **SH**, **X**, **Z**, and sometimes **CH**, you'll need to add **ES** to the end. Check out just a few of them now:

Plural mutants? Have they no shame? No matter—they will still be no match for Chi!

142

BUSINESS	**GAS**
INDEX	**FEZ**
TRENCH	**DISH**

Of course, this is only a tiny cross-section of the multitude of words that are made plural by adding **ES** to the end. Actually, almost all words ending in **O** are made plural by adding **ES**; we'll deal with the exceptions later. Take a look at a few of the **O** words that need **ES** to make them plural:

VETO	**TOMATO**
POTATO	**VOLCANO**

The last group of words that need **ES** to become plural are words ending in **F** or **FE**. However, there's a catch with most **F** and **FE** words. The final **F** or **FE** must be changed to **V** before the **ES** can be added. There are a few exceptions, but we'll deal with those later. Let's examine just a few of the **F** and **FE** words that fall under the **V** rule:

KNIFE	**HALF**
WIFE	**THIEF**

Granted, I'm the greatest Word Warrior of all time, but how the heck can I handle all these mutants at once, especially if they come in so many forms?

We've taken care of that for you, Chi. Our weapons specialists have a brand-new weapon for you designed specifically for the kind of mission you'll be facing here and on the next level. We have for you a nifty gadget called: the Pluralizer.

Sounds cool. What does it do?

When the Pluralizer is used on singular words, it makes them plural. In addition, the Pluralizer can be used to correct the spelling of mutants. It can turn singular mutants into correctly spelled plural nonmutants. As if that wasn't cool enough, the Pluralizer can also be used on plural mutants. When the Pluralizer is used on a plural mutant, the plural mutant becomes a correctly spelled nonmutant. The Pluralizer is one of the most powerful weapons to date. Why don't you give it a try? Use the Pluralizer to make the following words plural. Place the Pluralized words on the blanks next to the original words. When you have Pluralized all the words below, use the Appendix to check your work. We've done the first two for you.

Let's see what this baby can do!

BUSINESS	BUSINESSES	GAS	_____
KNIFE	KNIVES	HALF	_____
POTATO	_____	VOLCANO	_____
INDEX	_____	WAX	_____
WIFE	_____	THIEF	_____
VETO	_____	TOMATO	_____
TRENCH	_____	DISH	_____

Get Wise! Mastering Spelling Skills

Judging by your Pluralized words, the Pluralizer works precisely as it was designed to. Your ability to use new weapons flawlessly makes you the mutants' most formidable foe in the entire universe. Let's try that again. Same plan as last time but a new set of words:

ELF	_____	BUFFALO	_____
COMPLEX	_____	CALF	_____
MOSQUITO	_____	ZERO	_____
HELIX	_____	FUZZ	_____
LIFE	_____	LEAF	_____
HERO	_____	ECHO	_____
CRUNCH	_____	WISH	_____

Once again your Pluralizer performance is unparalleled! Outstanding work! Now for your challenge. For this mission, you'll need your Positron. Your Pluralizer needs to be recharged, so thankfully your toughest Pluralizer project isn't on this level. Here's the lowdown. Our researchers used the Pluralizer on some singular words and made them plural. However, the researchers used the Pluralizer on words that were unwittingly intermingled with mutants. Therefore, your mission is to use your Positron to identify the Pluralized words so that our extraction team can get them out of harm's way. You will need to look at the list on page 146 and then find their pluralized version in the star on page 147. Use a steady hand and do a great job! Just to be sure you got them all, check the key in the Appendix when you finish.

LUNCH	BOX
FORTRESS	GLASS
BUZZ	CRUSH
FOX	BUS
HERO	GROUCH
PUNCH	TORPEDO
BUSH	

I'm going in! I'll be so stealthy that the mutants won't even know I was there!

Get Wise! Mastering Spelling Skills

Level 23 Challenge

Complete the following puzzle challenge by identifying the correctly spelled pluralized words. These words are the plurals of the words found on page 146. Challenge solutions are in the Appendix.

```
                    Z
                 Z Z X
                 Y X F
               J U W F S
               L K V S B
             S E H C N U L
             X O Y S N Z N
           C V U D O S Z V H
           S T M S E H S U B
         S O K A O U P J V Z U
S Y G G L A S S S E R T R O F O R T R E S S E S S A L G B
 N L M B V Y E F E E E R D H Z O O E J E H C E H B V V
  G D U U U H O R H Q X F O A I E T V X Z S X O B I
   Z G G L C X D Q C T L B B P A O J O U T O F U
    X C R U S H E S N U U W T X Y Y B V W F O
    C G O N P L P H U J F F B F T D Q O L
      T R U C S B R C P Z Z D N H I V E
        G N C H U X O N R B S I U K C
        H N T H S D E T U S A H Q C L
        X B L D S A X Z O P S V U B G
        Y H D S A R T Z   I Y X S I T R M
        Z S S X C W E     K C G H Y X Q
      H K Q R A Z S         N P V I Z F A
      V J L P E Y           P Q K O K K
    U I I M W T             J O D W Y P
    B G Z E X               R M Z F Q
  Q J X Y Q                 R F R U H
  V E I O                   O K B B
W D G F                     S V N F
L Z                           F N
```

Our extraction team is in place and the Pluralized words are being rescued right now. Thanks to the Word Warrior, the universe is safe again, for a little while at least.

You have succeeded, and you may now advance to Level 24 for more Pluralizer action.

Level 24

The Pluralizer vs. the Exceptional Mutants

The evil scholars always try to stay one step ahead of the Word Warrior, and this level is no exception. Well, actually, this level is all about exceptions. You see, in the level you just completed, you dealt with plural forms of words that followed the rules— pretty basic stuff. Here, however, you will have to tackle all the mutants that are the *exceptions to the rules*. The evil scholars have named this group of mutants the "Exceptional Mutants" because they are just that—the *exceptions* to the rules. The evil scholars understand that the English language is as full of exceptions to rules as it is full of words that follow the rules. It is here, in the world of exceptions, that the evil scholars hope to strike at students and spellers, preying on their weaknesses.

The audacity of those guys! And they engineered an entire regiment of mutants just to take advantage of the exceptions to the rules? How vile!

This regiment of Exceptional Mutants has been programmed to break all the rules. The thing that makes this regiment dangerous is that they *seem* as if they should follow the rules, and that's where the deception comes in to play. For example, in the previous level you learned that an **ES** must be added to make a word plural when it ends in **O**. But there are a few exceptions to the **ES** rule. Take a look at the following list of some of these exceptions:

CONDO	**PIANO**
BRONCO	**SOLO**
STUDIO	**CAMEO**
CONCERTO	**PHOTO**

Each of these words is made plural by adding **S** *not* **ES**. The mutant plurals of the above words all have **ES** on the end just to confuse students. Likewise, you learned about the **F** words that have to be altered in order to become plural. Remember the **F** must be changed to **V** and then **ES** is added, like in the word HALVES? Well, the Exceptional Mutants would have you believe that that's *always* the case.

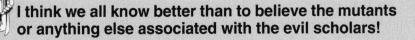

I think we all know better than to believe the mutants or anything else associated with the evil scholars!

Yes, Chi, but the mutants might be tough to identify if you aren't familiar with the exceptions to the **F** plural rule. Take a look at some of the words that are exceptions:

BELIEF	**BRIEF**
CHIEF	**KERCHIEF**
ROOF	**SPOOF**
GOOF	**PROOF**
STAFF	**SURF**
TURF	**DWARF**

To make each of these words plural, you simply add **S** to the end of the word. If you see one of these words that has had the **F** changed to **V** and then has **ES** on the end, you can be sure it's a mutant, one of the Exceptional Mutants, too.

Wow! Those guys sure are clever! They might have gotten me with one or two of those!

You aren't alone either, Chi. That's why it's so important that missions like this one are successful. Let's become a little more familiar with these exceptions. Take both of the lists and put them in alphabetical order in the blanks on the following page. This will help eliminate the possibility of you being tricked by the Exceptional Mutants. Just to be sure you did it correctly, check your work against the work in the Appendix.

1. _____ 2. _____ 3. _____

4. _____ 5. _____ 6. _____

7. _____ 8. _____ 9. _____

10. _____ 11. _____ 12. _____

13. _____ 14. _____ 15. _____

16. _____ 17. _____ 18. _____

19. _____ 20. _____

So far so good. Now we're gonna Pluralize these guys. Use your Pluralizer to make each of the following words plural. Place the Pluralized word in the blank next to the original word. Remember that the Pluralizer, when used correctly, will make any word properly plural even if it is an exception to the normal plural rules. Be sure to check your Pluralizer results against the results in the Appendix. The first one has been done for you.

BELIEF	BELIEFS	BRIEF	_____
CHIEF	_____	KERCHIEF	_____
ROOF	_____	SPOOF	_____
GOOF	_____	PROOF	_____
STAFF	_____	TURF	_____
SURF	_____	DWARF	_____
CONDO	_____	PIANO	_____
BRONCO	_____	SOLO	_____
STUDIO	_____	CAMEO	_____
CONCERTO	_____	PHOTO	_____

So far the Pluralizer has lived up to its billing, so the guys in the weapons lab probably deserve a raise! You now have the hang of Pluralizing these exceptions, so we need to get you involved in your mission without any further delays. Here's the scoop on your next mission: You're going to see a number of words below. Some are spelled correctly and some are mutants, Exceptional Mutants, that need to be Pluralized. In the blank next to each word, take the following actions. If the word is already spelled correctly, write **NPN** (short for No Pluralizing Necessary) in the blank next to the word. If the word is actually one of the Exceptional Mutants, Pluralize that sucker and put the new, Pluralized word in the blank. Remember that the fate of thousands, if not millions, of students throughout the universe is in your hands! Take careful aim, steady your hands, and Pluralize like there's no tomorrow! Check the results of the Pluralization in the Appendix after your mission.

Pluralize like there's no tomorrow? There is no tomorrow for those mutants!

BRONCOES	_____	BRIEFS	_____
CHIEVES	_____	PHOTOS	_____
ROOFS	_____	CONCERTOS	_____
PROOVES	_____	STAFFES	_____
SPOOVES	_____	TURFS	_____
SURVES	_____	PIANOES	_____
CONDOS	_____	DWARFS	_____
BELIEFS	_____	SOLOES	_____
STUDIOS	_____	CAMEOES	_____
GOOFES	_____	KERCHIEVES	_____

The Pluralizer and the Word Warrior come through again! The Exceptional Mutants have been permanently corrected and students are safe once again from the far-reaching grasp of the evil scholars.

Congratulations once again on a mission well done. Well, what are you waiting for? Go to Level 25!

Level 25

The Evil Scholars Strike Again

The evil scholars have outdone themselves this time with the mutants they engineered deep within that creepy laboratory. One thing hasn't changed, though. The evil scholars are still targeting words that students are already likely to confuse or misspell. This time the scholars have targeted words ending in **-ER, -OR**, and **-AR**. They genetically engineered droves of mutants to look like correctly spelled words just as they always have. These mutants take multiple forms, though. Let's take the word SCHOLAR, for example. Sometimes the mutant form of this word looks like SCHOLER and sometimes the mutant form of this word looks like SCHOLOR. Granted this is a potentially serious problem, but there is a lighter side to this new mutant discovery.

A lighter side to more mutants?

Yes, Chi, if you can believe it. Here's the funny thing about these new mutants. Our intelligence department has been intercepting tons of secret messages back and forth between the departments in the lab that read:

To: Scholers in the genetic engineering sector

and

To: Scholors in the virology sector

They probably had no idea that they were going to infect their own work when they created these **-ER, -OR**, and **-AR** mutants.

I guess it's true. Crime doesn't pay!

The interesting thing about the targeted words on this level is that there isn't a rule governing the correct spelling of the **-ER, -OR**, and **-AR** words. Never fear, though, because with a little practice and some Positron power, you'll be in good shape. Let's take a look at the first group of words, words all ending in **-ER:**

INTERPRETER	**BOOKKEEPER**
ADVERTISER	**EMPLOYER**

LABORER	**TREASURER**
MANUFACTURER	**CONSUMER**

Of course these aren't all the **-ER** words that might be misspelled, but these are the ones that have been mutated by the evil scholars. Now let's take a look at the **-OR** words that have been mutated. The archived list below is, of course, as the words appear in their original, *nonmutated* state:

CONTRACTOR	**AUTHOR**
SPECTATOR	**GOVERNOR**
ADMINISTRATOR	**OPERATOR**
INVESTIGATOR	**COUNSELOR**

The final group of words that have been mutated by the evil scholars for this level is below, and they all end in **-AR**. As with the first two lists, this is an archived list of what the correctly spelled words look like *before mutation*:

REGISTRAR	**PECULIAR**
CALENDAR	**OCULAR**
GRAMMAR	**SINGULAR**
PARTICULAR	**SIMILAR**

I can see how these could be tricky . . . If it weren't for my trusty Positron, that is!

Funny you should mention the Positron, Chi. We hope you have that handy because you'll need it pretty soon. But right now you'll need your writing implement. So that you'll become more familiar with the words that have been mutated, organize them into an alphabetical list; combine all three lists into one, alphabetized list. After you get them sorted, check your list against the list in the Appendix.

1. _____ 2. _____ 3. _____

4. _____ 5. _____ 6. _____

7. _____ 8. _____ 9. _____

10. _____ 11. _____ 12. _____

13. _____ 14. _____ 15. _____

16. _____ 17. _____ 18. _____

19. _____ 20. _____ 21. _____

22. _____ 23. _____ 24. _____

Great! Now it's time for the Positron! Below you will see a holographic image of the words from above. Each correctly spelled word will be grouped with two mutants. Use your Positron to positively identify each correctly spelled word by circling the right one in the group. Don't worry about the mutants—they're just holograms, for now. After you use the Positron on each word, check the Positronic results in the Appendix. We've done the first one for you.

The Princess of Positronic Power is ready to aim and fire!

INTERPRETER   BOOKKEEPAR   SPECTATOR

INTERPRETAR   BOOKKEEPER   SPECTATER

INTERPRETOR   BOOKKEEPOR   SPECTATAR

GOVERNER	LABOROR	TREASURAR
GOVERNOR	LABORER	TREASURER
GOVERNAR	LABORAR	TREASUROR
CONTRACTAR	AUTHAR	ADVERTISOR
CONTRACTER	AUTHER	ADVERTISER
CONTRACTOR	AUTHOR	ADVERTISAR
EMPLOYAR	PARTICULAR	SIMILER
EMPLOYOR	PARTICULER	SIMILAR
EMPLOYER	PARTICULOR	SIMILOR
MANUFACTUROR	CONSUMAR	CALENDAR
MANUFACTURER	CONSUMER	CALENDER
MANUFACTURAR	CONSUMOR	CALENDOR
OCULAR	ADMINISTRATER	OPERATAR
OCULER	ADMINISTRATAR	OPERATER
OCULOR	ADMINISTRATOR	OPERATOR
INVESTIGATOR	COUNSELOR	REGISTRER
INVESTIGATER	COUNSELAR	REGISTRAR
INVESTIGATAR	COUNSELER	REGISTROR
PECULIOR	GRAMMOR	SINGULOR
PECULIER	GRAMMAR	SINGULAR
PECULIAR	GRAMMER	SINGULER

Great Positronic work! Ready for the real thing? Good. This time it will be the real thing, not an exercise. Therefore, there is no margin for error if the evil scholars' latest plan is to be thwarted. Someone in our pyrotechnic department got a little trigger happy and dropped what was supposed to be a smart bomb into a crowded area full of mutants and nonmutants. It was supposed to knock out the **A**, the **E**, or the **O** from the **-AR**, **-ER**, and **-OR** endings of the mutant words.

But the smart bomb turned out to be a pretty dumb bomb because it knocked those letters out of all the words, mutants and nonmutants alike. Your job will be to use your writing implement to replace all the missing letters. Be very careful, though. If you replace the letters correctly, the new words will be permanently safe from any further mutation. However, if you put the wrong letter in a blank, the word will become a mutant, and we can't afford to have any more mutants running around, especially ones that we created! Complete your mission, then check your final results. Hopefully, you won't find any more mutants when you check your work in the Appendix!

REGISTR__R	PECULI__R	CALEND__R
OCUL__R	CONTRACT__R	AUTH__R
SPECTAT__R	GOVERN__R	INTERPRET__R
BOOKKEEP__R	ADVERTIS__R	EMPLOY__R
LABOR__R	TREASUR__R	MANUFACTUR__R
CONSUM__R	ADMINISTRAT__R	OPERAT__R
INVESTIGAT__R	COUNSEL__R	GRAMM__R
SINGUL__R	PARTICUL__R	SIMIL__R

Simply outstanding! You have reconstructed all the nonmutants, and you have prevented the reforming of any new mutants. Your mission was a total success!

Your work here was amazing, and you may now advance to Level 26.

Level 26

The Persia Virus

You won't believe the ridiculous lengths the evil scholars have gone to this time in their tireless quest to wreak havoc on the students and spellers across the universe. It seems that some historian with a twisted sense of humor has convinced the guys in the virology lab, the place where they engineer viruses, to create a really strange virus to attack normal words.

A historian? What the heck?

Sounds crazy, but here's the scoop. Apparently some crusty old historian who works for the evil scholars has some very old and very ancient ancestors from

Persia, the age-old rival of the ancient Greeks. Bear with us here. There is a point to this story. Believe it or not, this whacko historian has some grudge that's been in his family for centuries. He is holding this grudge against the ancient Greeks because his ancestors were upset that the English language is based on lots and lots of Greek words and not on Persian words. Seriously, could we make this stuff up?

So here's what this nut decided to do. He convinced the virology guys to create a virus that specifically targets and attacks words with Greek roots. He called it the Persia virus since the ancient Persians were constantly fighting the ancient Greeks.

If the Persia virus were to be successful in permanently altering words of Greek origin, the English language, not to mention all those who have to spell English words, simply would never be the same again.

Whoa! This is pretty serious! Do you think they would cancel the Olympics? What would Merriam-Webster do?

Yes, Chi, it's pretty darn serious. So that you can see just how serious this threat really is, you better have a look at some of the words that will be affected if the virus infects its targets. At the risk of you learning a little something extra, we've included some info on what each Greek root means; that may help you remember how to spell these words.

AGONY   **PROTAGONIST**   **ANTAGONIST**

from the Greek AGON, which means "struggle" or "control"

BICYCLE   **TRICYCLE**   **CYL**INDER

from the Greek CYCLOS, CYCL, or CYL, which means "wheel" or "circle"

MONOTONY   **MONO**TONOUS   **MONO**SYLLABLE

from the Greek MONO, which means "one"

EM**PATH**Y   SYM**PATH**Y

from the Greek PATH, which means "feeling"

STATIC   **STAT**US   THERMO**STAT**

from the Greek STAT, which means "to stand"

THERMAL   **THERM**OMETER   **THERM**OS

from the Greek THERM, which means "heat"

Wouldn't it be weird if the virus attacked things that were from GEEKS instead of from the GREEKS?

So that you become more familiar with the targets of this heinous campaign against Greek words, read through the following list of words and keep your writing implement handy. As you read each word, rewrite the word in the blank next to the word. When you rewrite each word, though, write the Greek root in ALL CAPS so that during your mission you'll recognize these words as having Greek roots. The first one has been done for you as an example. Be sure to double-check your work with the Appendix.

THERMAL	THERMal	EMPATHY	_____
AGONY	_____	MONOSYLLABLE	_____
THERMOS	_____	BICYCLE	_____
STATIC	_____	SYMPATHY	_____
STATUS	_____	MONOTONOUS	_____
THERMOSTAT	_____	THERMOMETER	_____
ANTAGONIST	_____	MONOTONY	_____
CYLINDER	_____	PROTAGONIST	_____
TRICYCLE	_____		

Superb! You are truly the master of the writing implement! Your skills are unparalleled in all the universe! Is this a shameless attempt to butter you up for your next exercise? Maybe. Regardless, it's very important that the Greek-based words above be organized alphabetically so that you have a great reference tool for your mission. Using your highly touted writing implement, alphabetize the words in the blanks on the next page. Be sure to check your list against the one in the Appendix. By the way, did you know that the word ALPHABETIZE is based on the Greek words APLHA and BETA, the first two letters of the Greek alphabet?

I do now!

1. _____ 2. _____ 3. _____

4. _____ 5. _____ 6. _____

7. _____ 8. _____ 9. _____

10. _____ 11. _____ 12. _____

13. _____ 14. _____ 15. _____

16. _____ 17. _____

Truly masterful! There is no doubt that you're ready for the final challenge. Here's the nitty-gritty. The Persia virus has indeed infected some of these words. However, not all of the words have been infected. The ones that have been infected must be placed in a special place so that the virus will be destroyed and the words returned to normal. Believe it or not, the one thing that can destroy the Persia virus is Greek food. After you read each infected, or misspelled, word, you need to place the word in the Giant Gyro Machine below it, correctly spelled of course. Again, could we really make this stuff up? Got it? Go get 'em! Check your gyro, uh, your answers in the Appendix upon completion of your mission.

I'm getting hungry. Any chance you have some baklava lying around?

Across

2. antaganist
3. empothy
7. manasyllable
8. thurmal
9. manatony
11. cilinder
12. stadus
13. stadic
14. bycycle

Down

1. agany
4. protaganist
5. thurmostat
6. manatonous
10. trycycle

Level 26 Challenge

Complete the following puzzle challenge by correctly spelling the words with Greek roots and placing them into the Gyro Machine. Challenge solutions are in the Appendix.

GIANT GYRO MACHINE

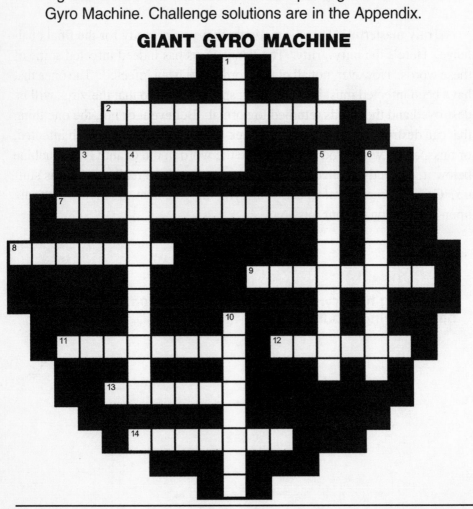

Get Wise! Mastering Spelling Skills

Fantastic! The words are resting comfortably inside the Giant Gyro Machine, and they should be completely recovered very shortly! The Greeks and Geeks alike thank you for your tireless efforts in this fight against evil!

Congratulations on another fine effort. Do not stop by a Greek delicatessen but rather advance directly to Level 27.

Level 27

Munchable Mutants?

The evil scholars have come up with some outrageous schemes so far, but their latest plot may outdo all of them. You know, playing mind games is pretty low. Striking the hearts of students is lower. Striking at students' stomachs, though, has to be the lowest of the low. That's right. The evil scholars have cooked up a whole host of mutants designed specifically to confuse students when they try to spell some tricky words related to food and eating.

Sounds like a *recipe* for disaster!

Well put, Chi. These guys have certainly sunk to new depths. If the evil scholars were successful in scattering these mutants throughout the universe, students would be in big trouble (not to mention *really* hungry!). But that's not the worst of it. Those students might grow up never knowing the true spellings of these words. Moreover, just think of all the misspelled menus, shopping lists, and recipes across the universe—all thanks to those darn scholars and their mutants. There is so much riding on this that only the Word Warrior can get the job done.

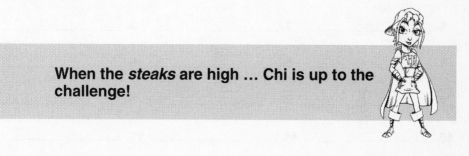

When the *steaks* are high ... Chi is up to the challenge!

Thank goodness! This is one of the most serious threats yet. To see just how big a threat this actually is, check out the list of words that the scholars have cloned and then genetically engineered in order to make things difficult for everyone. Read through the list, and just look at the unsuspecting words that have been infected by the heinous villains:

NAUSEOUS	RASPBERRY
CANTALOUPE	RESTAURANT
CHOCOLATE	PROTEIN
PISTACHIO	GUACAMOLE
SHISH KEBAB	CALORIE
BARBECUE	MARSHMALLOW
REFRIGERATOR	SANDWICH
CELERY	DAIQUIRI
LASAGNA	APPETIZER
DESSERT	CARBOHYDRATE

If you get too hungry, and you start to lose your focus, just look back at the first word in the list. Before we see how dastardly these scholars are, let's get the words sorted out so that they are a little more organized and easy to study. Use your writing implement and organize these words into an alphabetical list. As you're organizing the words, try to figure out what all these words have in common besides the fact that they are all related to Chi's favorite pastime outside of mashing mutants. Check your work against the menu in the Appendix.

1. _____ 2. _____ 3. _____

4. _____ 5. _____ 6. _____

7. _____ 8. _____ 9. _____

10. _____ 11. _____ 12. _____

13. _____ 14. _____ 15. _____

16. _____ 17. _____ 18. _____

19. _____ 20. _____

Did you see the pattern?

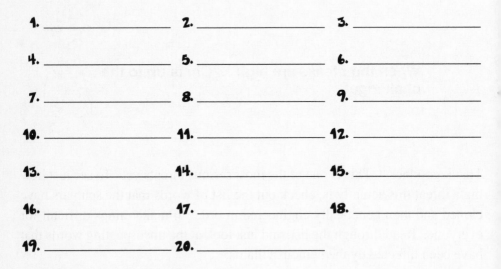

Those scholars knew exactly what they were doing when they cooked up this batch of mutants.

Now go back and read the list out loud. Go on. Nobody's watching you . . . Now that wasn't so bad, was it? Did you notice that almost all of these words, when pronounced, have some issues? Some words have letters that are silent.

Some have letters that seem like they should be single instead of doubled and vice-versa. Some of the words just aren't spelled the way they sound. We told you those evil scholars were clever! So, to help you identify the trouble spots and reinforce the correct spellings of these words in your mind, read through the list below and use your writing implement to fill in the missing letters and complete the words.

I got it. Just stuff the empty words with the letters needed to make each word well done and spelled to perfection! Be sure to check the ingredients in the Appendix when you're done.

CEL__RY

NAUS_____S

CANTAL____PE

PISTA____IO

DE____ERT

SH__SH K__BAB

BARBE__UE

CAL__RIE

CHOC__LATE

LASA__NA

D____QUIRI

RAS__BERRY

REST____RANT

GUACAMOL__

CARBOH__DRATE

REFRIGERAT__R

MARSHM__LLOW

SAN__WICH

PROT____N

A____ETIZER

Good work! We're ready for you to jump right into your challenge and get these mutants out of the frying pan and into the fire. Our intelligence agents have located the entire group of mutants that have been cloned to look like the words from our lists. Oddly enough, the real words are in the same place. We've located all the words *and* mutants in a shopping cart in a local grocery store. Your mission is to sort out the mess in the shopping cart and identify all twenty of the real words with your Positron. After you ID them, get out of there as quickly as you can! Our secret agent is disguised as the bag boy at the grocery store. He'll place the real words in paper bags and the mutants in plastic bags after they go through checkout. Then our other secret agent disguised as, you guessed it, a carry-out boy will properly recycle the plastic bags full of mutants. Got it? Great! Don't forget to check the contents of your bag with the brown paper bag in the Appendix.

Let's kick it up a notch and get cooking!

Level 27 Challenge

Complete the following puzzle challenge by identifying and then circling the correctly spelled words. Challenge solutions are in the Appendix.

SHOPPING CART

```
                                    X                        F
                                    Y                L O    P
                                    N                Y O R  F
                                    V              U T J W

  I R I U Q I A D Y Z N R I Y J O I E R C C A G E I
X Y N A O R I R G A R E K C Y W Y H C H J E F N L
F L A D S Y B U D R Z R L R Q H Y S O T T L E Q A
F H X D R P G S E I E N E O G K H C L A D L U C S
B O H E B P B S T T W U I B M I L A L E F R Q R A
R I L S U E T E A K Q A O E S A S O S T E R E B G
I E V S B A P R R A J B A H T A C E R M W Z B F N
C U F E U P E E D R I G K E N O R A A I I S R N A
Y B B R A G I J Y K Y E F Y H T R R U T X R A A U
G R A T I R D I H O B R A C S Y S P T G A L B U S
K N E R O G H S O A E M A R S H M E L L O W L S E
T O F L B X E D B S W P H I M K P I S T A S H I O
H E A E A E H R R P T N U A R A T S E R O Z P O U
R C I N H C C A N T A L O U P E F U Q I H D U S
H F T S D T I U C T M L L Y L O M A C A U G T S G
H I B I P D W G E H O O I H C A T S I P A M V K A
D Q C W H D S O W V R Q C Z M N Z P T M D L Y
        N N                      A C
        U B A G                  T A C K
        V H S S                  K Y W W
        Z P Q A                  M E V H
        T K                      F T
```

Well, Chi, thanks to you, this one's in the bag! Now go have a snack.

Stick a fork in this level—it's done! You may now advance to Level 28.

Level 28

The Persia Virus: Second Verse, Worse than the First

We *really* thought we got rid of the Persia virus. But apparently the evil scholars released the second wave of the virus at about the same time you were vanquishing the *first* Persia virus. This strain of the Persia virus has all the characteristics of the first strain, but according to the latest intelligence reports, it is more resistant to disinfectants, antidotes, etc. Our research department will have to work overtime to come up with a strategy for handling these mutants. While they're working on that, you'd better have a look at the latest batch of innocent words with Greek roots mutated by the evil scholars.

BIOLOGY   **BIO**SPHERE

from the Greek BIO, which means "life"

GENEALOGY   **GENE**TICS

from the Greek GENE, which means "birth"

SYNONYM   **SYN**C   **SYN**THESIS

from the Greek SYN, which means "together"

PHONICS   TELE**PHON**E

from the Greek PHON, which means "sound"

AUTOMATIC   **AUTO**MATION   **AUTO**BIOGRAPHY

from the Greek AUTO, which means "self"

GRAPHIC   PHONO**GRAPH**   TELE**GRAPH**

from the Greek GRAPH, which means "to write"

OPTICAL   **OPT**OMETRY

from the Greek OPT, which means "sight"

NAUTICAL   ASTRO**NAUT**

from the Greek NAUT, which means "sailor" or "traveler"

These words were carefully selected because the main thing they have in common is a Greek root.

That's it? That just sounds nasty, bleak, and absolutely hopeless . . . There aren't even any spelling rules or *anything* else that can help us on this mission?

No, Chi. We are sorry, but we are relying on your vast experience, your quick wits, and your spelling prowess, all of which you have been absorbing into that mental container on top of your body since you've picked up this book.

Huh? It *is* lonely at the top.

Here's another look at the list. As you read each word, use your writing implement to reproduce the word in the blank next to the word. When you do, make the Greek root ALL CAPS. The first one has been done for you already. Be sure to double-check your work with the Appendix.

BIOLOGY   ___*BIOlogy*___   BIOSPHERE   _____

GENEALOGY   _____   GENETICS   _____

SYNONYM   _____   SYNC   _____

SYNTHESIS   _____   PHONICS   _____

TELEPHONE _____   AUTOMATIC _____

AUTOMATION _____   AUTOBIOGRAPHY _____

GRAPHIC _____   PHONOGRAPH _____

TELEGRAPH _____   OPTICAL _____

OPTOMETRY _____   NAUTICAL _____

ASTRONAUT _____

Excellent use of the writing implement! You should be teaching a class on how to use that thing! Before you put it away, however, you'll need it one more time to get these words alphabetized. Be sure to check your alphabetical list against the one in the Appendix. Did we mention that the word *alphabet* . . .

Yeah, yeah. Comes from the Greek letters ALPHA and BETA. Thanks for the reminder, though.

1. _____   2. _____   3. _____

4. _____   5. _____   6. _____

7. _____   8. _____   9. _____

10. _____   11. _____   12. _____

13. _____   14. _____   15. _____

16. _____   17. _____   18. _____

19. _____

Awesome alphabetizing! You're ready for battle now. If you recall, the mutants on Level 26 were defeated by Greek food, of all things. These mutants, unfortunately, are a little nastier, a little meaner, and *a lot* more resistant to this treatment. In addition, the mutants have now multiplied! And, if that weren't enough, the mutants have captured all the original words and are on their way back to the lab with them. We'll try to detain them for a while, but you need to help with the search-and-rescue mission. Use your Positron to circle the innocent words, and we'll send our sweeper team to take care of the mutants. Do be careful out there, and make sure your work is correct by using the Appendix to verify the Positronic results. We've done the first one for you.

> **The Pontiff of the Positron is ready for action! Innocents, here I come! Mutants, your time is almost up!**

BIOLLOGY	BIASPHERE	GENEOLOGY
BIOLIGY	BIOSPHERE	GENIALOGY
(BIOLOGY)	BIOSFERE	GENEALOGY
GENNETICS	SYNONYM	SYNC
GENETICS	SYNANYM	SINC
GENETTICS	SYNYNYM	SYNK
SYNTHESIS	PHONNICS	TELLEPHONE
SINTHESIS	PHONICS	TELEPHONE
SYNTHYSIS	PHONIX	TELLIPHONE

AUTOMATTIC	AUTOMATION	AUTOBYOGRAPHY
AUTOMATIC	AUTOMMATION	AUTABIOGRAPHY
AUTAMATIC	AUTAMATION	AUTOBYOGRAPHY
GRAFFIC	PHONNOGRAPH	TELIGRAPH
GRAFIC	PHONOGRAPH	TELEGRAPH
GRAPHIC	PHONAGRAPH	TELLEGRAPH
OPTOCAL	OPTOMMETRY	NAUTICAL
OPTACAL	OPTOMETRY	NAUTTICAL
OPTICAL	OPTOMYTRY	NAUTYICAL
ASTRONOT		
ASTRONAUT		
ASTRAUNOT		

Your Positronic identification of the innocent words is second to none! The sweeper team is in position now, and eradication of the mutants will commence as soon as we have the innocents at a safe distance from the action. Those scholars should, perhaps, check into getting some new historians. As everyone knows, the Persians never conquered the Greeks!

There was never any doubt in *my* mental container that the Persia virus was going down. You may now proceed to Level 29.

Sowing the Seeds of Chaos

Now that we have ruined the evil scholars' "**i** before **e** except after **c**" myth, they have now devised one of the most clever misinformation campaigns ever. They call it the "Seeds of Chaos." These "seeds" are, of course, our mutant rebels and not real seeds. These mutants have been carefully designed to confuse students when they meet up with words that end in:

-SEED   **-SEDE**   **-CEDE**

Actually, there aren't very many words that end in these suffixes, but they tend to give students quite a bit of trouble. With those darn mutants still running around, this situation is very likely to become worse. Take a look at the following list of words that have been targeted by the scholars and their mutant friends.

So they think they're farmers now, huh? Seeds of Chaos! Let me at 'em!

SUPERSEDE	**INTERCEDE**
EXCEED	**SUCCEED**
SECEDE	**ACCEDE**
RECEDE	**PROCEED**
PRECEDE	**CONCEDE**
BIRDSEED	**CEDE**
HAYSEED	

Did you notice that SUPERSEDE is the only word that ends in **-SEDE**? Basically, there are two simple rules, which if you take a moment to store away in your brain, will guarantee accurate spelling, as well as the positive identification of mutants:

★ SUPERSEDE is the only word that ends in **-SEDE**. So, if you see any other word ending in **-SEDE**, you can be *sure* that it's a mutant.

★ EXCEED, SUCCEED, and PROCEED are the only words that end in **-CEED**. Any other word ending in **-CEED** is a mutant.

Something interesting to note is that SEED and CEDE are both suffixes *and* words that can stand alone. On the other hand, **-CEED** and **-SEDE** are *not* words but suffixes only. Another trick that will help keep these words straight is organizing them into an alphabetized list. Use your writing implement to alphabetize these words, and be sure you check the list with the alphabetized list in the Appendix.

1. _____ 2. _____ 3. _____

4. _____ 5. _____ 6. _____

7. _____ 8. _____ 9. _____

10. _____ 11. _____ 12. _____

13. _____

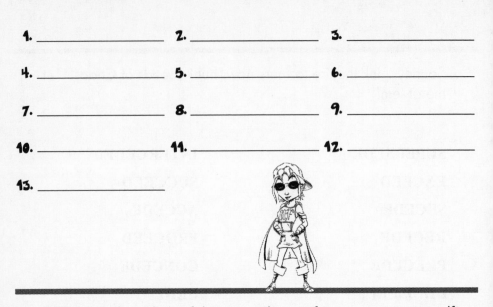

Sensational seeding of these words . . . if I may say so, myself!

Yes, you're probably getting the hang of these words, but a little more practice is in order just to make sure that you are ready for the final challenge. Now, set your Positron to circle, and then use it to choose the correctly spelled word from each of the pairs on the following page. Relax and do a good job. There are no real mutants here in our practice session, just some holographic images of the Seeds of Chaos mutants. Check your Positronic results with those in the Appendix. We've done the first one for you.

So while there is no real danger, I know I'll need this practice for the final challenge. Practice makes perfect, you know!

SUPERSEDE	INTERCEED
(SUPERCEDE)	INTERCEDE
EXCEDE	SUCCEDE
EXCEED	SUCCEED
SECEED	ACCEED
SECEDE	ACCEDE
RECEED	PROCEDE
RECEDE	PROCEED
PRESEED	CONCEDE
PRECEDE	CONSEED
BIRDSEED	CEED
BIRDSEDE	CEDE
HAYCEDE	
HAYSEED	

The Positron comes through again and delivers a flawless performance! We've come to expect nothing less than Positronic perfection from you.

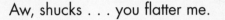

Aw, shucks . . . you flatter me.

Now that you've mastered these words, it's time for our real confrontation with the Seeds of Chaos. Coming up is the final challenge which, of course, you must master before you can move on to the next and final level.

Our intelligence agents located the mutants and blasted them to bits. But, it would be a shame to waste all those word parts. Therefore, we need you to reconstruct the word parts and create new words from the old mutant parts. From the jumbled mess below, select a word part *and* a suffix that make a word, of course, and then place them together in the Word Cementing Chamber so the two word parts can permanently bond. Feel free to use your writing implement to cross them out as you go.

Just to give you a little head start, we've dropped a few clues into the Word Cementing Chamber. You should check the results in the Appendix when you're done. Do a great job on your final challenge and don't accidentally fall into the Cementing Chamber!

HAY	-SEDE	-CEDE	-CEDE	SUPER
EX	-CEED	PRE	-CEED	INTER
SUC	-SEED	-CEDE	-CEED	SE
RE	-CEDE	PRO	AC	
-CEDE	CON	-CEDE		
BIRD	-SEED	-CEDE		

Level 29 Challenge

Complete the following puzzle challenge by placing a word part and its correct suffix together from the list on page 184 into the chamber. Challenge solutions are in the Appendix.

WORD CEMENTING CHAMBER

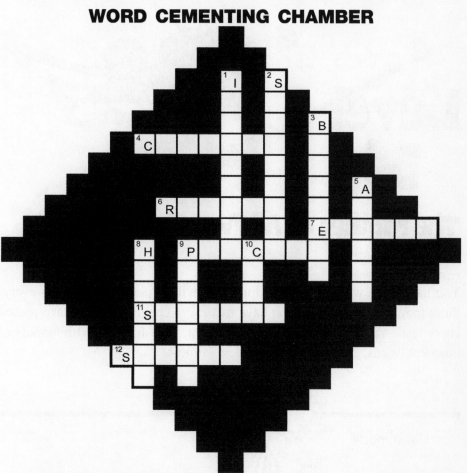

Looks like we have successfully weeded out all the mutants and got these words off to a flying new start! Outstanding work! The Seeds of Chaos never stood a chance against the Word Warrior!

Two green thumbs way up on a job well done! You may now advance to Level 30!

Level 30

The Mother of All Final Challenges

You have done well, Word Warrior. The evil scholars have thrown everything they had at you, and you have met *every* challenge. You have passed *every* test. You have defeated *every* mutant. You have saved hundreds of innocent words. You have done it all . . . almost.

Uh, almost?

That's right. You have *almost* done it all. You have one challenge left, one final, final challenge. Have you ever watched a horror movie on TV? Go ahead and fess up. Everyone has watched *Carrie* or *Halloween*. When you were watching, did you notice how the evil monster always found a way to get back up and make a final stand? How do they do that? We don't know, but we have good reason to believe that the evil scholars know.

The evil scholars watch TV?

Maybe, but that's not the point. This is the point. Somehow, the evil scholars have found a way to organize an *entire army of mutants* for one last final stand against the Word Warrior. In this, the Mother of All Final Challenges, you must draw on all the knowledge you have gained throughout the 29 previous levels. And, you must complete the Mother of All Final Challenges in order to be completely victorious. Are you up to it?

Am *I* up to it? Are the scholars evil? Are the mutants slimy? Am I not the Word Warrior of renown, celebrity, and legend throughout the universe and of all time?

Okaaaay. But perhaps your victories have gone to your head just a wee bit now. So slow down, because now here's the first part of the Mother of All Final Challenges. You will see a list of mutants. Take the proper measures to correct each of the mutant words, then carefully place the corrected words in the Antimutant Holding Cells. These Antimutant Holding Cells will strip the former mutants of all remaining mutant DNA, leaving only a corrected, fully functional, properly spelled word.

Be careful, though, because you are dealing with mutants from any number of our 29 previous levels. In addition, these mutants are in no order at all. You'll have to summon all your wits and word power to be successful here.

However, since you are dealing with so many mutants from so many different levels, a clue about the mutant has been provided for each mutant. The clues will provide you with the level on which you first encountered the mutant. Therefore, if you need to refer back to that level for a spelling rule or a hint, you can do so. When you finish this part of the challenge, be sure you verify the results in the Appendix. Take a deep breath, get focused, and start whacking those mutants.

Across

5. ACHIEVEING (Level 2)

9. SOLEM (Level 4)

10. SUFOCATE (Level 5)

11. UTILISE (Level 6)

12. INUENDO (Level 5)

Down

1. COMGRESS (Level 3)

2. LOVEABLE (Level 1)

3. CHASTIZE (Level 6)

4. CONFUSEION (Level 2)

6. DEBATEABLE (Level 1)

7. INDETTED (Level 4

8. INMUNITY (Level 3)

Level 30/Challenge 1

Complete the following puzzle by correctly spelling each word on page 188 and placing it in Antimutant Holding Cell 1. Challenge solutions are in the Appendix.

ANTIMUTANT HOLDING CELL 1

Wow! You handled those mutants with ease! However, don't get too sure of yourself because they will surely get tougher as you progress through to the final challenge. Do not let down your guard. Just when you least expect it, those evil scholars will try to throw you a curve.

Throw the Word Warrior a curve, and I'll hit it out of the park!

That's exactly the kind of confidence you should have now after completing so many levels and final challenges. Take that confidence and attack these mutants the way you did the first group of mutants. Now, when you look at the list below, you'll see that every word is a mutant. Take corrective action on the mutants, and then carefully place them into Antimutant Holding Cell 2. Please be sure that you don't accidentally place a mutant in a cell. That could be disastrous.

Corrective action? I'm gonna *manhandle* those mutants!

Across

1. SIGNIFIGANT (Level 11)
3. SEKWEL (Level 10)
5. KWIVER (Level 10)
8. SLIEGH (Level 9)
9. ELECANT (Level 11)
10. ISOLATEION (Level 7)
11. JEWLRY (Level 12)

Down

2. ILUMINATE (Level 8)
3. SUFICIENT (Level 8)
4. CREATEION (Level 7)
6. RIENDEER (Level 9)
7. FEBUARY (Level 12)

Level 30/Challenge 2

Complete the following puzzle by correctly spelling each mutant word on page 190 and placing it in Antimutant Holding Cell 2. Challenge solutions are in the Appendix.

ANTIMUTANT HOLDING CELL 2

You called it! Those manhandled mutants are history! Your mutant-mashing abilities are awesome! It's a good thing too, because you won't even have time to catch your breath before you have to battle the next wave of mutants. Here they come! Break a leg!

Across

4. RACOON (Level 18)

5. CAFFIENE (Level 17)

7. LIESURE (Level 17)

8. ALLYANCE (Level 16)

9. DETECTIBLE (Level 16)

11. PARRALLEL (Level 14)

12. TIMLY (Level 13)

Down

1. AMUSMENT (Level 13)

2. PERNOUNCE (Level 14)

3. HOSTELL (Level 15)

6. CAPATAL (Level 15)

10. AGRIEVED (Level 18)

Level 30/Challenge 3

Complete the following puzzle by correctly spelling each mutant word from the previous page and placing it in Antimutant Holding Cell 3. Challenge solutions are in the Appendix.

ANTIMUTANT HOLDING CELL 3

Three down, two to go, and so far so good. It seems like the Word Warrior's power continues to grow with every phase of the final challenge. Is the Mother of All Final Challenges all it's cracked up to be?

Are you kidding? So far this is the Munchkin of All Final Challenges! I expected more from the evil scholars!

Well, Chi, you want more? You got it! The evil scholars are stepping it up a notch in this phase of the final challenge. In this phase, you'll see a series of sentences. Hiding in each sentence are two mutants. Your job is twofold. First, use your Positron to identify the mutants in each sentence. Second, you'll need to use your writing implement to write the correct spellings of the mutated words in the blanks after each sentence. Can you handle that? Let's hope so. It's up to you and your brain power. We've done . . . well, you know that!

Level 30 Challenge 4

1. My sisterinlaw claims she's thirtyfour years old, but she's been making that claim for as long as I can remember. (Level 19)

   ___sister-in-law___   ___thirty-four___

2. Charlie has some of the worst handwriting I've ever tried to read, and I think that's because he's both far-sighted and lefthanded. (Level 19)

   _____   _____

3. Which would you rather do: circlenavigate the globe in a balloon or make a trancecontinental trip on a bicycle? (Level 20)

_____   _____

4. That guy is so hiperactive that he had to sign up for every intermural sport just so he could burn some energy. (Level 20)

_____   _____

5. It appears that the runaway Russian satelite is on a colision course with our school cafeteria. Bummer. (Level 21)

_____   _____

6. Why is it that guys in movies with metalic teeth always turn out to be the vilain? (Level 21)

_____   _____

7. I would make a terrible politician because I always get panicy when I have to start politicing and speaking in public places. (Level 22)

_____   _____

8. His nose was so zincy from all the sunblock that he smeared on his face that he looked like someone shellaced his nose with plaster. (Level 22)

_____   _____

9. The football player ate so many bratwursts that his stomach filled with gasses and his belches sounded like volcanos. (Level 23)

_____   _____

10. Which food is used most often in soup: tomatos or potatos? (Level 23)

_____   _____

11. He thinks he plays concertoes beautifully on the pianoes in the music store in the mall, but everyone cringes when he plays. (Level 24)

_____   _____

12. I tried to take some photoes of the condoes where we stayed during Spring Break, but just like with every other picture I tried to take, I accidentally left the lens cap on the camera. (Level 24)

_____   _____

Surely you jest! That's the best that the scholars can come up with? They have no chance at ruling the universe!

Well, you sure did a number on those mutants! We knew you were good, but maybe we underestimated just how unbelievable you really are! OK, we're convinced, but you still have one more group to convince that you are totally unstoppable: The evil scholars and their last group of mutants! This is it. The final phase of the Mother of All Final Challenges. This is the last stand and the fate of the universe hangs in the balance. Defeat these mutants and students everywhere can finally sleep well tonight. Fail to defeat the mutants and . . . well we don't want to even think about the consequences. You must prevail. We all have our fingers crossed, and we're pulling for you.

Enough of the ra-ra speech, already! Give me the stuff I need to know!

Very well! These mutants are especially deceptive. They have scrambled themselves in an attempt to go undetected. Therefore, your job is twofold. First, you have to unscramble the mutants. Just set your writing implement to "descramble." Place the descrambled mutant in the blank under each mutant. Keep in mind that the unscrambled mutant will still be a misspelled mutant; you're job is to remove the letter that is incorrect.

The second step in the process is to take corrective action and place the final corrected word in the proper Antimutant Holding Cell. Only when this has been completed can we all breathe a collective sigh of relief. We're counting on you!

Counting on me? Ever wonder why it's not "We're *spelling* on you?"

Across

3. CREEDSUPE (Level 29)

_____

5. REPSTACTE (Level 25)

_____

7. MEOWSHRLALM
(Level 27)

_____

8. DROPEES (Level 29)

_____

Down

1. STINSHESI (Level 28)

_____

2. METEORMORTH (Level 26)

_____

3. PYMSHIAT (Level 26)

_____

4. GLYOOGENE (Level 28)

_____

5. CHERSOL (Level 25)

_____

6. RICELEA (Level 27)

_____

Final Challenge

Complete the following puzzle by correctly spelling the words on page 197 and placing in Antimutant Holding Cell 4 . Challenge solutions are in the Appendix.

ANTIMUTANT HOLDING CELL 4

Get Wise! Mastering Spelling Skills

By George, I think you've got it. You've really got it. It's done! The mutants have finally all been eliminated. The universe is now safe for students and spellers alike!

Wait! What about the evil scholars and their lab?

We forgot to tell you! While you were completing the final phase of the Mother of All Final Challenges, the evil scholars turned themselves in to the authorities! For their crimes against vocabulary, they are facing numerous charges including:

★ **Disturbing the Ps**

★ **K-napping**

★ **M-bezzlement**

★ **Assault and batter-E**

★ **X-tortion**

★ **And more**

By the time they get out of jail, you'll be an English teacher!

Then be afraid. Be very afraid.

Congratulations! You've successfully completed not only 29 levels of spelling challenges but also the Mother of All Final Challenges. Keep your E-Zapper, your E-Plenisher, your Positron, your IONizer, and all your other gadgets handy because you never know when you'll need them. Also, keep your eyes open because you also never really know when you'll see another mutant—for some strange reason, they show up on tests a lot.

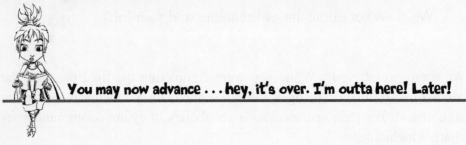

You may now advance . . . hey, it's over. I'm outta here! Later!

Appendix

Level 1

Page 3

PLEASURABLE

DESIRABLE

LIKABLE

BELIEVABLE

ADVISABLE

LIVABLE

VALUABLE

ARGUABLE

USABLE

EXCUSABLE

ADMIRABLE

PROVABLE

LOVABLE

DEBATABLE

MOVABLE

Page 5

MANAGEABLE

ENFORCEABLE

NOTICEABLE

REPLACEABLE

KNOWLEDGEABLE

EXCHANGEABLE

EXCUSABLE

TRACEABLE

SERVICEABLE

Page 6

1. ADMIRABLE
2. ADVISABLE
3. ARGUABLE
4. BELIEVABLE
5. CHANGEABLE
6. DEBATABLE
7. DESIRABLE
8. ENFORCEABLE
9. EXCHANGEABLE
10. EXCUSABLE
11. KNOWLEDGEABLE
12. LIKABLE
13. LIVABLE
14. LOVABLE
15. MANAGEABLE
16. MOVABLE
17. NOTICEABLE
18. PLEASURABLE
19. PROVABLE
20. REPLACEABLE
21. SERVICEABLE
22. TRACEABLE
23. USABLE
24. VALUABLE

Get Wise! Mastering Spelling Skills

Level 2

Page 10

ACHING

SEVERITY

USING

REVERSIBLE

CONFUSION

ARRIVAL

COMPLETING

ACHIEVING

ADVISOR

GUIDANCE

AMUSING

RESEMBLANCE

PROPOSAL

IGNITION

REHEARSAL

Page 11

1. ACHIEVING
2. ACHING
3. ADVISOR
4. AMUSING
5. ARRIVAL
6. COMPLETING
7. CONFUSION
8. GUIDANCE
9. IGNITION
10. PROPOSAL
11. REHEARSAL
12. RESEMBLANCE
13. REVERSIBLE
14. SEVERITY
15. USING

Page 12

1. LOVABLE
2. ACHING
3. ARRIVAL
4. AMUSING
5. IGNITION
6. SEVERITY
7. PROPOSAL

Level 3

Page 15

CONGRESSIONAL

IMMORTALITY

COMPROMISE

IMMUNITY

INNOCENT

CONSERVATIVE

INTUITION

IMBEDDED

CONNOTATION

COMMENTATOR

IMMEDIATELY

IMPATIENT

IMMACULATE

INSULATION

COMBUSTION

COMPETITION

COMMERCIAL

IMPOSTOR

IMPEACH

Page 16

1. COMBUSTION
2. COMMENTATOR
3. COMMERCIAL
4. COMPETITION
5. COMPROMISE
6. CONGRESSIONAL
7. CONNOTATION
8. CONSERVATIVE
9. IMBEDDED
10. IMMACULATE
11. IMMEDIATELY
12. IMMORTALITY
13. IMMUNITY
14. IMPATIENT
15. IMPEACH
16. IMPOSTOR
17. INNOCENT
18. INSULATION
19. INTUITION

Page 17

INPOSTER CHAOS

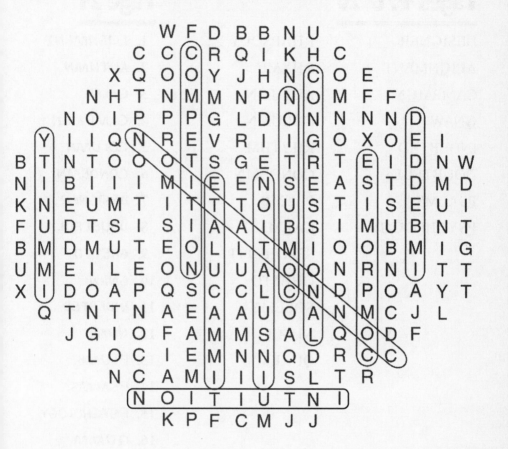

Level 4

Pages 19 & 20

DESI**G**NER

ALI**G**NMENT

CAMPAI**G**N

GNAW

INDE**B**TED

DOU**B**TFUL

PSALMS

PSYCHOLOGY

R**H**APSODY

R**H**YME

AUTUM**N**

COLUM**N**

R**H**YTHM

CONDEM**N**

PLUM**B**

CAL**M**

SPA**G**HETTI

G**H**ETTO

SOLEM**N**

NUM**B**

QUA**L**M

Page 21

1. ALIGNMENT

2. AUTUMN

3. CALM

4. CAMPAIGN

5. COLUMN

6. CONDEMN

7. DESIGNER

8. DOUBTFUL

9. GHETTO

10. GNAW

11. INDEBTED

12. NUMB

13. PLUMB

14. PSALMS

15. PSYCHOLOGY

16. QUALM

17. RHAPSODY

18. RHYME

19. RHYTHM

20. SOLEMN

21. SPAGHETTI

Page 22

DEBRIEFING CELLS

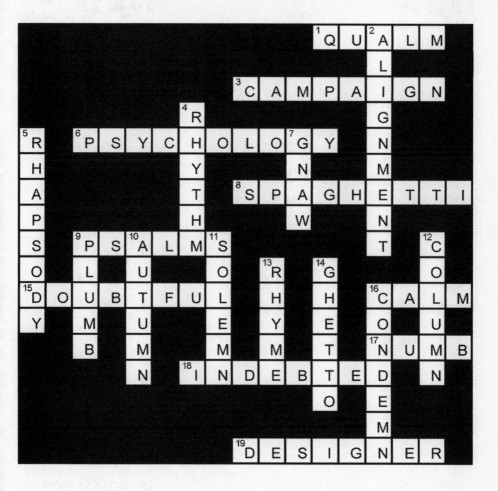

Level 5

Page 26

INNOCUOUS

COLOSSAL

DISSIPATE

HARASS

HARASSMENT

NECESSARY

POSSESS

POSSESSION

ASSESS

ASSESSMENT

CASSEROLE

ASSASSIN

INNUENDO

QUESTIONNAIRE

TYRANNY

BATTALION

SUFFOCATE

COLLAPSE

CORRESPOND

OFFICIAL

BROCCOLI

SUCCESS

Page 27

1. ASSASSIN
2. ASSESS
3. ASSESSMENT
4. BATTALION
5. BROCCOLI
6. CASSEROLE
7. COLLAPSE
8. COLOSSAL
9. CORRESPOND
10. DISSIPATE
11. HARASS
12. HARASSMENT
13. INNOCUOUS
14. INNUENDO
15. NECESSARY
16. OFFICIAL
17. POSSESS
18. POSSESSION
19. QUESTIONNAIRE
20. SUCCESS
21. SUFFOCATE
22. TYRANNY

Page 28

INNOCUOUS
COLOSSAL
DISSIPATE
HARASS
HARASSMENT
NECESSARY
POSSESS
POSSESSION
ASSESS
ASSESSMENT
CASSEROLE

ASSASSIN
INNUENDO
QUESTIONNAIRE
TYRANNY
BATTALION
SUFFOCATE
COLLAPSE
CORRESPOND
OFFICIAL
BROCCOLI
SUCCESS

Page 30

1. TYRANNY
2. NECESSARY
3. DISSIPATE
4. BATTALION
5. INNOCUOUS
6. COLOSSAL
7. CASSEROLE
8. QUESTIONNAIRE

Page 33

CAPITALIZE	CRITICIZE
ADVISE	ADVERTISE
CAPSIZE	SANITIZE
UTILIZE	VISUALIZE
IMPROVISE	CHASTISE
ORGANIZE	DESPISE
DEVISE	SUPERVISE
REVISE	EXERCISE
AUTHORIZE	AGONIZE
SURPRISE	RECOGNIZE

Page 34

1. ADVERTISE
2. ADVISE
3. AGONIZE
4. AUTHORIZE
5. CAPITALIZE
6. CAPSIZE
7. CHASTISE
8. CRITICIZE
9. DESPISE
10. DEVISE
11. EXERCISE
12. IMPROVISE
13. ORGANIZE
14. RECOGNIZE
15. REVISE
16. SANITIZE
17. SUPERVISE
18. SURPRISE
19. UTILIZE
20. VISUALIZE

Page 35

MUTANT MASH

Level 7

Page 40

EQUATION

SEPARATION

NARRATION

IRRITATION

EVALUATION

CREATION

COORDINATION

ISOLATION

DESECRATION

OBLIGATION

DECORATION

GRADUATION

INFILTRATION

INSTITUTION

GENERATION

PARTICIPATION

Page 40

1. COORDINATION

2. CREATION

3. DECORATION

4. DESECRATION

5. EQUATION

6. EVALUATION

7. GENERATION

8. GRADUATION

9. INFILTRATION

10. INSTITUTION

11. IRRITATION

12. ISOLATION

13. NARRATION

14. OBLIGATION

15. PARTICIPATION

16. SEPARATION

Page 42

DEBRIEFING CELLS

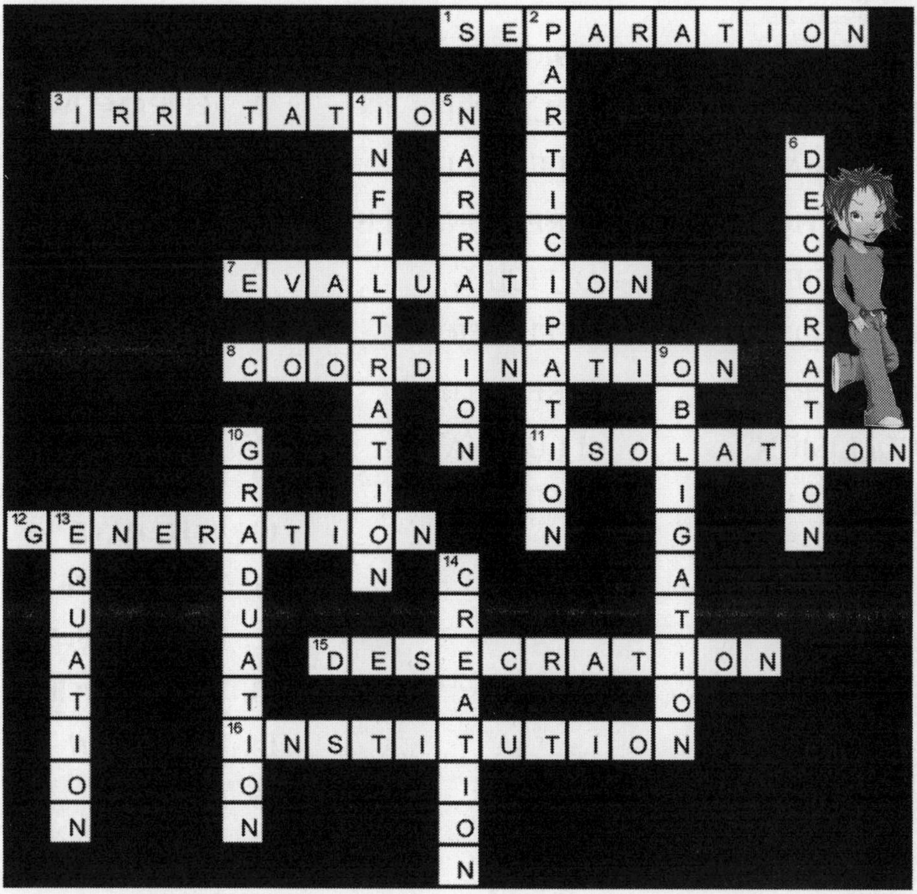
1 SEPARATION
2 PARTICIPATION
3 IRRITATION
4 INFILTRATION
5 NARRATION
6 DECORATION
7 EVALUATION
8 COORDINATION
9 OBLIGATION
10 GRADUATION
11 ISOLATION
12 GENERATION
13 EQUATION
14 CREATION
15 DESECRATION
16 INSTITUTION

Level 8

Page 45

AFFORD

IRRIGATION

AFFIRMATIVE

AFFECTION

SUFFICIENT

OFFERED

CORRUPT

COLLISION

ILLITERATE

CORRESPONDENT

COLLAPSE

ILLEGIBLE

IRRESPONSIBLE

OFFICIAL

AFFLICTION

IRRESISTIBLE

ILLUMINATE

Page 46

1. AFFECTION
2. AFFIRMATIVE
3. AFFLICTION
4. AFFORD
5. COLLAPSE
6. COLLISION
7. CORRESPONDENT
8. CORRUPT
9. ILLEGIBLE
10. ILLITERATE
11. ILLUMINATE
12. IRRESISTIBLE
13. IRRESPONSIBLE
14. IRRIGATION
15. OFFERED
16. OFFICIAL
17. SUFFICIENT

Page 47

AFFORD	CORRESPONDENT
IRRIGATION	COLLAPSE
AFFIRMATIVE	ILLEGIBLE
AFFECTION	IRRESPONSIBLE
SUFFICIENT	OFFICIAL
OFFERED	AFFLICTION
CORRUPT	IRRESISTIBLE
COLLISION	ILLUMINATE
ILLITERATE	

Page 48

AFFORD	CORRESPONDENT
IRRIGATION	COLLAPSE
AFFIRMATIVE	ILLEGIBLE
AFFECTION	IRRESPONSIBLE
SUFFICIENT	OFFICIAL
OFFERED	AFFLICTION
CORRUPT	IRRESISTIBLE
COLLISION	ILLUMINATE
ILLITERATE	

Level 9

Page 51

1. COUNTERFEIT
2. FEIGN
3. FOREIGN
4. FOREIGNER
5. FORFEIT
6. FREIGHT
7. HEINOUS
8. NEIGH
9. NEIGHBOR
10. REIGN
11. REIN
12. REINDEER
13. SEINE
14. SLEIGH
15. SOVEREIGN
16. SURFEIT
17. THEIR
18. VEIL
19. VEIN
20. WEIGH
21. WEIGHT

Page 53

EXTRACTION ARENA

```
                  M B P
              K Q M M F G U E H
            Y K I I T O M Z X F Y E H
        W B R S N Y R X H B E C Y E Y U Y
        C M I E E H I S X B C E L X U D J C H
      O O Z E T E I F R O F R T R K T B N J L
      S N J U D G J D E U L N X R U U H F H C W
      J P F G G N U H C N V G G N O C B M Y G R I K
      B Q E G E E T L T N I E G H B O R H I B H Z Y
      U P G W R I I M E E W E I G H T W Y F K G S P K
      U C I B H E R R E R T I A R L G K I E K D D I R V
      W Q U X F N F M E G F J E S P I I Z S S U V E Z B
      M H H M R R E R V V V V I S X B E Q C G J F K Y A U N
      O B Q O X I I O L S F O R E I G N E R K D Z E B Q F J
      F P F Y T E S U G I V S B T N H C X K C X I D B F A
      R F D H G U F P K S U P L H G V B F F V P E J V P
      D E T T H R P H E R U D A I I A D S K F Z F Z I K
      O Y I E T F K I F C S S E E E B F M M Y M Z N Q
      E X G O I N E H Z P L L R F G M F A K I K M K
      N D I H E I N O U S X M S M U H H L H J G R Y
        I D I T E O H X E K W B H C T N X R R V D
      N V A Y V U F C V S P D W F I K R I R W F
      W Q K M S J M Y M S O T G M U V S L A
      K R C P P M G T H P L D V R V L C
          N T G G C X W C T E X R U
            K I U M D C Q E I
                P F Q
```

Level 40

Page 57

UNIQUE <u>CK</u>

CLIQUE <u>CK</u>

PLAQUE <u>CK</u>

MASQUERADE <u>CK</u>

CONQUER <u>CK</u>

LACQUER <u>CK</u>

ACQUIRE <u>KW</u>

ADEQUATELY <u>KW</u>

QUARANTINE <u>KW</u>

SEQUEL <u>KW</u>

QUINTUPLET <u>KW</u>

QUAINT <u>KW</u>

QUENCH <u>KW</u>

BANQUET <u>KW</u>

ACQUAINTED <u>KW</u>

QUIZZICAL <u>KW</u>

COLLOQUIAL <u>KW</u>

QUIVER <u>KW</u>

INQUISITIVE <u>KW</u>

QUESTIONNAIRE <u>KW</u>

Page 58

UNIQUE

CLIQUE

PLAQUE

MASQUERADE

CONQUER

LACQUER

ACQUIRE

ADEQUATELY

QUARANTINE

SEQUEL

QUINTUPLET

QUAINT

QUENCH

BANQUET

ACQUAINTED

QUIZZICAL

COLLOQUIAL

QUIVER

INQUISITIVE

QUESTIONNAIRE

Page 59

1. ACQUAINTED

2. ACQUIRE

3. ADEQUATELY

4. BANQUET

5. CLIQUE

6. COLLOQUIAL

7. CONQUER

8. INQUISITIVE

9. LACQUER

10. MASQUERADE

11. PLAQUE

12. QUAINT

13. QUARANTINE

14. QUENCH

15. QUESTIONNAIRE

16. QUINTUPLET

17. QUIVER

18. QUIZZICAL

19. SEQUEL

20. UNIQUE

Level 10 (continued)

Page 60

MUTANT-PROOF FORCEFIELD

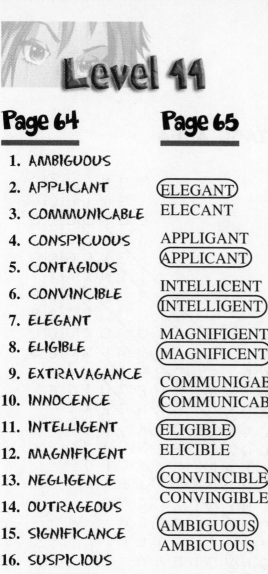

Level 44

Page 64

1. AMBIGUOUS
2. APPLICANT
3. COMMUNICABLE
4. CONSPICUOUS
5. CONTAGIOUS
6. CONVINCIBLE
7. ELEGANT
8. ELIGIBLE
9. EXTRAVAGANCE
10. INNOCENCE
11. INTELLIGENT
12. MAGNIFICENT
13. NEGLIGENCE
14. OUTRAGEOUS
15. SIGNIFICANCE
16. SUSPICIOUS

Page 65

(ELEGANT)
ELECANT

APPLIGANT
(APPLICANT)

INTELLICENT
(INTELLIGENT)

MAGNIFIGENT
(MAGNIFICENT)

COMMUNIGABLE
(COMMUNICABLE)

(ELIGIBLE)
ELICIBLE

(CONVINCIBLE)
CONVINGIBLE

(AMBIGUOUS)
AMBICUOUS

(INNOCENCE)
INNOGENCE

(NEGLIGENCE)
NEGLICENCE

SIGNIFIGANCE
(SIGNIFICANCE)

(EXTRAVAGANCE)
EXTRAVACANCE

OUTRACEOUS
(OUTRAGEOUS)

(SUSPICIOUS)
SUSPIGIOUS

(CONTAGIOUS)
CONTACIOUS

(CONSPICUOUS)
CONSPIGUOUS

Level 11 (continued)

Page 67

HOSTAGE AREA

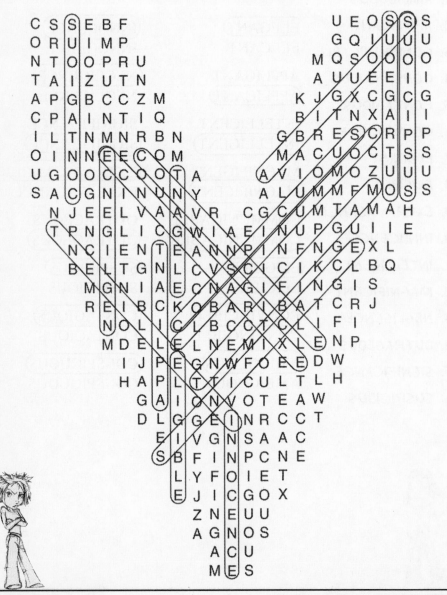

Level 42

Page 72

SOPHOMORE

COMFORTABLE

POSTPONE

QUANTITY

ET CETERA

ENVIRONMENT

GOVERNOR

WEDNESDAY

JEWELRY

WHISTLE

KITCHEN

BUDGET

HANDSOME

RECOGNIZE

GOVERNMENT

FEBRUARY

ELEMENTARY

ENTERTAINMENT

Page 73

1. BUDGET

2. COMFORTABLE

3. ELEMENTARY

4. ENTERTAINMENT

5. ENVIRONMENT

6. ET CETERA

7. FEBRUARY

8. GOVERNMENT

9. GOVERNOR

10. HANDSOME

11. JEWELRY

12. KITCHEN

13. POSTPONE

14. QUANTITY

15. RECOGNIZE

16. SOPHOMORE

17. WEDNESDAY

18. WHISTLE

Page 75

HOLDING CELLS

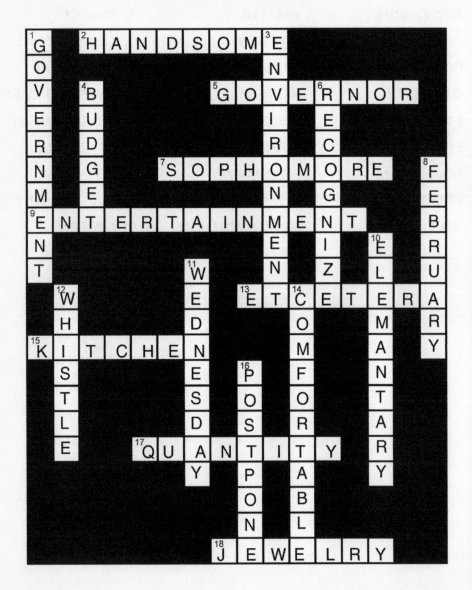

Level 43

Page 79

MERELY
LONELY
TIMELY
LOVELY
SINCERELY
LIKELY
IMMEDIATELY
SEVERELY
COMPLETELY
DEFINITELY

SENSELESS
PRICELESS
ENGAGEMENT
STATEMENT
AMUSEMENT
CONFINEMENT
MEASUREMENT
ADVERTISEMENT
INTENSELY

Page 80

1. ADVERTISEMENT
2. AMUSEMENT
3. COMPLETELY
4. CONFINEMENT
5. DEFINITELY
6. ENGAGEMENT
7. IMMEDIATELY
8. INTENSELY
9. LIKELY
10. LONELY
11. LOVELY
12. MEASUREMENT
13. MERELY
14. PRICELESS
15. SENSELESS
16. SEVERELY
17. SINCERELY
18. STATEMENT
19. TIMELY

Level 13 (continued)

Pages 80 & 81

MER<u>E</u>L_Y

LON<u>E</u>L_Y

TIM<u>E</u>L_Y

LOV<u>E</u>L_Y

SINCER<u>E</u>L_Y

LIK<u>E</u>L_Y

IMMEDIAT<u>E</u>L_Y

SEVE_R<u>E</u>LY

COMPLE_T<u>E</u>LY

DEFINIT<u>E</u>L_Y

SEN_S<u>E</u>LESS

PRIC<u>E</u>L_ESS

ENGA_G<u>E</u>MENT

STAT<u>E</u>M_ENT

AMU_S<u>E</u>MENT

CONFIN<u>E</u>M_ENT

MEASUR<u>E</u>M_ENT

ADVERTIS<u>E</u>M_ENT

INTENS<u>E</u>L_Y

Level 44

Page 84

RECESSION	PROFESSION
PROCESSION	UNNECESSARY
CONCESSION	UNCONSCIOUS
CONSTITUTION	PRONOUNCE
PERSUADE	MISSPELL
DISSUADE	PARALLEL
INTERMISSION	PERSEVERANCE
PROPORTION	PERFORATED
DISSATISFIED	PERENNIAL
PERMISSION	SUBCOMMITTEE

Page 85

1. CONCESSION
2. CONSTITUTION
3. DISSATISFIED
4. DISSUADE
5. INTERMISSION
6. MISSPELL
7. PARALLEL
8. PERENNIAL
9. PERFORATED
10. PERMISSION
11. PERSEVERANCE
12. PERSUADE
13. PROCESSION
14. PROFESSION
15. PRONOUNCE
16. PROPORTION
17. RECESSION
18. SUBCOMMITTEE
19. UNCONSCIOUS
20. UNNECESSARY

Level 14 (continued)

Page 86

(RECESSION)	RECCESSION	RECESION
PROFFESION	(PROFESSION)	PROFESION
PROCCESSION	PROCESION	(PROCESSION)
UNNECCESSARY	UNECESSARY	(UNNECESSARY)
(CONCESSION)	CONCESION	CONNCESSION
(UNCONSCIOUS)	UNCONCIOUS	UNCONNSCIOUS
CONSTITUON	CONSTUTUTION	(CONSTITUTION)
PORNOUNCE	(PRONOUNCE)	PRONNOUNCE
PROSUADE	PURSUADE	(PERSUADE)
(MISSPELL)	MISPELL	MISPPELL
(DISSUADE)	DISUADE	DISSUDE
(PARALLEL)	PARRALLEL	PARRALEL
INTROMISSION	INTRAMISSION	(INTERMISSION)
PERSERVERANCE	(PERSEVERANCE)	PRESEVERANCE
(PROPORTION)	PORPORTION	PURPORTION
(PERFORATED)	PORFORATED	PERFERATED
(DISSATISFIED)	DISATISFIED	DISSATIFIED
PERRENNIAL	PERRENNIAL	(PERENNIAL)
PERMISION	PERMISSIN	(PERMISSION)
SUBCOMITEE	SUBCOMMITEE	(SUBCOMMITTEE)

Level 45

Page 91

ISLE

CAPITOL

COMPLIMENT

DISSENT

FOWL

HORDE

HOSTILE

PRINCIPLE

REVUE

STATIONERY

VILE

Page 92

HORDE

CAPITAL

VILE

DISSENT

COMPLIMENT

ISLE

FOWL

REVIEW

PRINCIPLE

HOSTILE

HOARD

STATIONERY

STATIONARY

PRINCIPAL

VIAL

AISLE

HOSTEL

REVUE

FOUL

CAPITOL

COMPLEMENT

DESCENT

Level 15 (continued)

Pages 93 & 94

1. The travelers sought refuge in the small ~~hostile~~ **HOSTEL** just off the highway.

2. The hunters observed dozens of species of ~~foul~~ **FOWL**, but they never saw the elusive dodo bird.

3. The bride tripped as she walked down the (AISLE), the groom knew he would get in trouble later, but he laughed out loud anyway!

4. The clever car salesman knew that the way to get big sales was to dish out big ~~complements~~ **COMPLIMENTS**.

5. The (STATIONARY) bike is the most boring exercise machine in the gym, besides the treadmill, the rowing machine, the stair-master, and the ab machine.

6. The ~~vial~~ **VILE** little man never sends birthday cards to his family.

7. Our drama department's spring (REVUE) was absolutely spectacular!

8. The ~~principle~~ **PRINCIPAL** gave me lunch detention for six weeks for putting worms in her spaghetti.

9. There's no need to (HOARD) the peanuts; my little brother already sucked all the chocolate off of them anyway!

10. The winning candidate was shocked to learn that the loser rolled the (CAPITOL) with toilet paper after the election results were finalized.

11. As he started his ~~dissent~~ **DESCENT** down the stairs, he tripped over his shoelace, tumbled down the stairs, and became the laughingstock of the school.

Get Wise! Mastering Spelling Skills

Level 46

Page 98

1. ACCEPTABLE
2. ACCEPTANCE
3. ADJACENT
4. ALLIANCE
5. APPEARANCE
6. APPROACHABLE
7. ATTENDANCE
8. CLEARANCE
9. COMPATIBLE
10. COMPLIANCE
11. CONFIDENCE
12. CONFIDENT
13. DEPENDABLE
14. DEPENDANCE
15. DETECTABLE
16. EXPERIENCE
17. IGNORANCE
18. IMPOSSIBLE
19. INCREDIBLE
20. INDEPENDENCE
21. INGREDIENT
22. OBTAINABLE
23. PERMANENT
24. PERMISSIBLE
25. PROMINENT
26. RESEMBLANCE
27. SUPERINTENDENT
28. SUSCEPTIBLE

Page 99

COMPAT**IBLE**

CLEAR**ANCE**

SUSCEPT**IBLE**

DETECT**ABLE**

PERMISS**IBLE**

SUPERINTEND**ENT**

ATTEND**ANCE**

INDEPEND**ENCE**

RESEMBL**ANCE**

CONFID**ENCE**

Level 16, page 99 (continued)

APPROACHABLE

IMPOSSIBLE

OBTAINABLE

INCREDIBLE

APPEARANCE

EXPERIENCE

DEPENDABLE

INGREDIENT

ACCEPTABLE

COMPLIANCE

PERMANENT

ALLIANCE

CONFIDENT

IGNORANCE

ADJACENT

DEPENDENCE

PROMINENT

ACCEPTANCE

Level 47

Page 103

1. CAFFEINE

2. CEILING

3. CONCEITED

4. CONCEIVE

5. DECEIT

6. DECEIVE

7. EITHER

8. FAHRENHEIT

9. HEIGHT

10. INVEIGLE

11. LEISURE

12. NEITHER

13. PERCEIVE

14. PROTEIN

15. RECEIPT

16. RECEIVE

17. SEIZE

18. SEIZURE

19. WEIRD

Page 103

(RECEIVE) RECIEVE

RECIEPT (RECEIPT)

(CEILING) CIELING

CONCIEVE (CONCIEVE)

CONCIETED (CONCEITED)

(DECEIVE) DECIEVE

DECIET (DECEIT)

(PERCEIVE) PERCIEVE

(SEIZE) SIEZE

IETHER (EITHER)

NIETHER (NEITHER)

(PROTEIN) PROTIEN

SIEZURE (SEIZURE)

(WEIRD) WIERD

(HEIGHT) HIEGHT

(LEISURE) LIESURE

CAFFIENE (CAFFEINE)

(FAHRENHEIT) FAHRENHIET

(INVEIGLE) INVIEGLE

Page 105

```
J W A I J X C F
B H H T I L R M K
N E G T V L I K N O
M Y Z S X E U E P B G
S E K P H M I Z S V X
I T U Z U T N U G U V B
F P P S H O R T P X R Z
G V R E C I E V E I C E D
B L R O I E H R R S X P K G A P C Z O T J U
R   H P D I T C T Q C T B J F D Y W B E I V I K O
X S T W E G N Y E E N I E F F A C T E V E I C N O C A
G D J U O B G H R I R E Z I S H T O R H N O L V E   L N
G E S X D F F Y U N N V E U V R V E N O N K S I X   Q T
G I B P X C F V Z Z W E I R D E T E I C N O C E N S D R H F
M   V G L J Z I I R P S L L N R D E C E I T G I G R B G A
    Z K L W D E U M T A K D H U I N V E I G L E Z P L I W
T   Q Q A S R S Q M X P Q A I V A I L B D T E V I E C E D
K P R J Y N D I A V C A F F I E N E I T O R P E R U U S H
R F W O H C E W A I J C V Y G T C N R G Y H V S D L S
H O D G U L J C C G K J O H I E G H T H R Q I S Y U
A X T J Y I N F D D U I O V R A
M   S O P L I P L B E E U M
    D H D N A E G H C Z F W
    I H F E C Q Z K E B J
    H B J W L E S I Y Q C
    Y Z E V Z K S M V E
    T F Y H F A F D Q Y
    A M S F J W W H K
    B I U K Q C I J F
    B J S J F S L A
```

SHIP OF DEC*I*EVERS

Level 48

Page 109

CO**RR**OBORATE

I**MM**ACULATE

MAYO**NN**AISE

A**GG**RAVATE

CO**NN**OI**SS**EUR

STA**CC**ATO

A**CC**UMULATE

A**CC**OST

A**GG**RE**SS**IVE

A**CC**LAIM

A**CC**O**MM**ODATE

RA**CC**OON

A**CC**ORDION

A**GG**RIEVED

A**CC**OMPLISH

Page 110

1. ACCLAIM

2. ACCOMMODATE

3. ACCOMPLISH

4. ACCORDION

5. ACCOST

6. ACCUMULATE

7. AGGRAVATE

8. AGGRESSIVE

9. AGGRIEVED

10. CONNOISSEUR

11. CORROBORATE

12. IMMACULATE

13. MAYONNAISE

14. RACCOON

15. STACCATO

Page 111

CORR**R**OB__ORATE

IM**M**AC__ULATE

MAYON**N**AIS__E

AG**G**RAV__ATE

CON**N**OISSEUR__

STAC**C**AT__O

A**C**CUM__ULATE

A**C**COS__T

AG**G**R__ESSIVE

AC**C**L__AIM

AC**C**OMMOD__ATE

R__AC**C**OON

AC**C**ORD__ION

AG**G**RIEV__ED

AC**C**OM__PLISH

Page 112

Level 49

Page 117

1. BACKGROUND
2. BOOKEEPER
3. COPYRIGHT
4. ELSEWHERE
5. FARSIGHTED
6. GRANDMOTHER
7. GRANDPARENT
8. GREAT-UNCLE
9. GREAT-GRANDPARENTS
10. LEFT-HANDED
11. LONG-TERM
12. NEARSIGHTED
13. NEWSROOM
14. NEWSSTAND
15. NOWHERE
16. PLAYGROUND
17. PLAYWRIGHT
18. RIGHT-HANDED
19. ROOMMATE
20. SEVENTY-ONE
21. SISTER-IN-LAW
22. TEAMMATE
23. THREE-FIFTHS
24. TWENTY-THREE
25. TWO-THIRDS
26. WHOEVER

Pages 118 & 119

(TWO-THIRDS)   THREEFIFTHS
TWOTHIRDS   (THREE-FIFTHS)

TWENTYTHREE   SEVENTYONE
(TWENTY-THREE)   (SEVENTY-ONE)

(BACKGROUND)   PLAY-GROUND
BACK-GROUND   (PLAYGROUND)

(ELSEWHERE)   NO-WHERE
ELSE-WHERE   (NOWHERE)

NEWS-STAND   NEWS-ROOM
(NEWSSTAND)   (NEWSROOM)

ROOM-MATE   (TEAMMATE)
(ROOMMATE)   TEAM-MATE

(PLAYWRIGHT)   (COPYRIGHT)
PLAY-WRIGHT   COPY-RIGHT

WHO-EVER
(WHOEVER)

(BOOKKEEPER)
BOOK-KEEPER

GRAND-MOTHER
(GRANDMOTHER)

GRAND-PARENT
(GRANDPARENT)

(LONG-TERM)
LONGTERM

(SISTER-IN-LAW)
SISTERINLAW

NEAR-SIGHTED
(NEARSIGHTED)

(FARSIGHTED)
FAR-SIGHTED

RIGHTHANDED
(RIGHT-HANDED)

LEFTHANDED
(LEFT-HANDED)

Page 122

Without Hyphens	With Hyphens
GRANDMOTHER	TWO-THIRDS
GRANDPARENT	THREE-FIFTHS
WHOEVER	TWENTY-THREE
BOOKKEEPER	SEVENTY-ONE
COPYRIGHT	SISTER-IN-LAW
PLAYWRIGHT	RIGHT-HANDED
TEAMMATE	LEFT-HANDED
ROOMMATE	
NEWSSTAND	
NEWSROOM	
NOWHERE	
ELSEWHERE	
PLAYGROUND	
BACKGROUND	
NEARSIGHTED	
FARSIGHTED	

Level 20

Page 125

1. ANTECEDENT
2. ANTISPETIC
3. CIRCUMNAVIGATE
4. CIRCUMSCRIBE
5. HYPERACTIVE
6. HYPOTHESIS
7. INTERCOLLEGIATE
8. INTERVIEW
9. INTRAMURAL
10. INTRAVENOUS
11. PERMEATE
12. PERSPIRE
13. SUPERFICIAL
14. SUPERINTENDENT
15. TRANSCONTINENTAL
16. TRANSLUCENT

Page 126

TRANS ~~INTER~~LUCENT

HYPO ~~INTER~~THESIS

ANTE ~~PER~~CEDENT

SUPER ~~INTRA~~FICIAL

ANTI ~~TRANS~~SEPTIC

PER ~~SUPER~~SPIRE

INTRA ~~CIRCUM~~MURAL

CIRCUM ~~HYPER~~NAVIGATE

PER ~~ANTE~~MEATE

INTER ~~HYPO~~VIEW

TRANS ~~ANTI~~CONTINENTAL

HYPER ~~CIRCUM~~ACTIVE

CIRCUM ~~INTRA~~SCRIBE

SUPER ~~PER~~INTENDENT

INTER ~~TRANS~~COLLEGIATE

INTRA ~~SUPER~~VENOUS

Page 127

CIRCUMNAVIGATE	ANTECEDENT
TRANSLUCENT	SUPERINTENDENT
CIRCUMSCRIBE	ANTISEPTIC
TRANSCONTINENTAL	HYPERACTIVE
INTERVIEW	SUPERFICIAL
HYPOTHESIS	INTRAVENOUS
INTERCOLLEGIATE	PERSPIRE
PERMEATE	INTRAMURAL

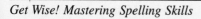

Level 24

Page 131

1. ALLEGIANCE
2. ALLOTMENT
3. ALLUDE
4. ALLURE
5. BALLOON
6. COLLABORATE
7. COLLISION
8. COLLUSION
9. ELLIPSE
10. METALLIC
11. MISCELLANEOUS
12. OSCILLATE
13. PARALLEL
14. SATELLITE
15. SKILLFUL
16. VILLAIN

Pages 131 & 132

COLLISION

ALLURE

BALLOON

VILLAIN

COLLABORATE

SKILLFUL

PARALLEL

ALLEGIANCE

SATELLITE

COLLUSION

OSCILLATE

ALLUDE

ELLIPSE

MISCELLANEOUS

ALLOTMENT

METALLIC

Page 133

ANTIVIRAL DISINFECTANT AREA

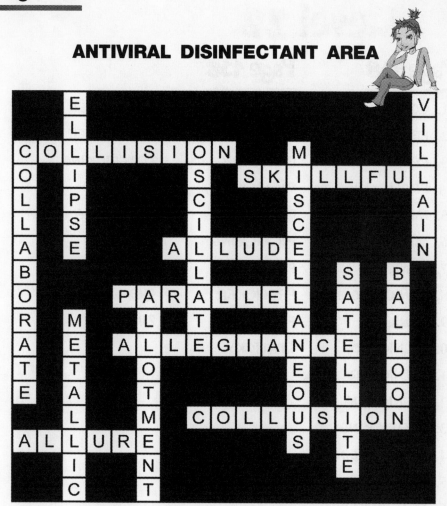

Level 22

Page 138

Page 138

1. COLICKY
2. FROLICKED
3. FROLICKER
4. FROLICKING
5. MIMICKED
6. MIMICKING
7. PANICKED
8. PANICKING
9. PANICKY
10. PICNICKED
11. PICNICKER
12. PICNICKING
13. POLITICKING
14. SHELLACKED
15. STATICKY
16. TRAFFICKED
17. TRAFFICKER
18. TRAFFICKING
19. ZINCKY

PANICKY
PANICKED
PANICKING
PICNICKED
PICNICKER
PICNICKING
FROLICKED
FROLICKER
FROLICKING
STATICKY

TRAFFICKED
TRAFFICKER
TRAFFICKING
MIMICKED
MIMICKING
COLICKY
POLITICKING
SHELLACKED
ZINCKY

Page 140

LIQUIFIED VITAMIN K POOL

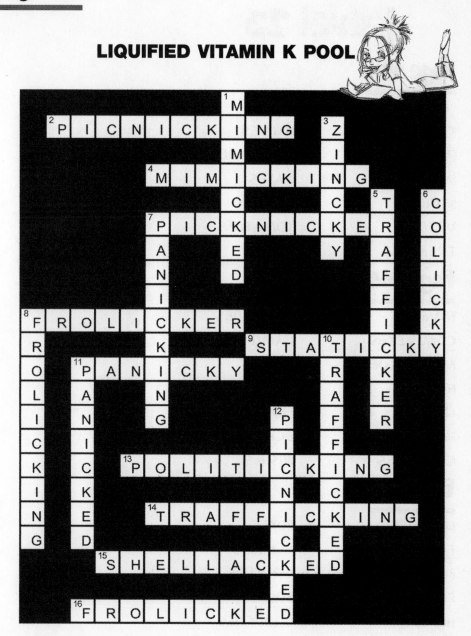

Level 23

Page 144

BUSINESSES

KNIVES

POTATOES

INDEXES

WIVES

VETOES

TRENCHES

GASES

HALVES

VOLCANOES

WAXES

THIEVES

TOMATOES

DISHES

Page 145

ELVES

COMPLEXES

MOSQUITOES

HELIXES

LIVES

HEROES

CRUNCHES

BUFFALOES

CALVES

ZEROES

FUZZES

LEAVES

ECHOES

WISHES

Page 146

LUNCHES

FORTRESSES

BUZZES

FOXES

HEROES

PUNCHES

BUSHES

BOXES

GLASSES

CRUSHES

BUSES

GROUCHES

TORPEDOES

Get Wise! Mastering Spelling Skills

Page 147

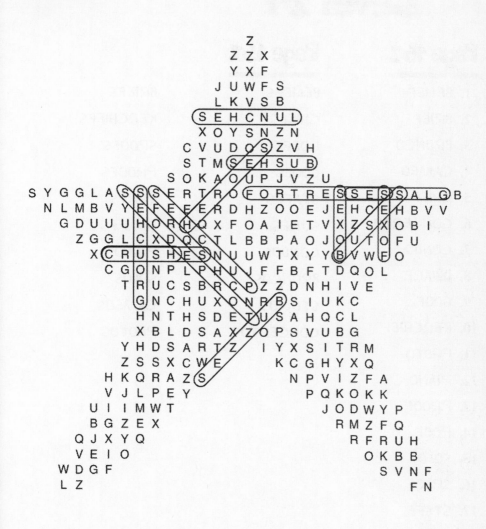

Level 24

Page 152

Page 152

1. BELIEF
2. BRIEF
3. BRONCO
4. CAMEO
5. CHIEF
6. CONCERTO
7. CONDO
8. DWARF
9. GOOF
10. KERCHIEF
11. PHOTO
12. PIANO
13. PROOF
14. ROOF
15. SOLO
16. SPOOF
17. STAFF
18. STUDIO
19. SURF
20. TURF

BELIEFS
CHIEFS
ROOFS
GOOFS
STAFFS
SURFS
CONDOS
BRONCOS
STUDIOS
CONCERTOS

BRIEFS
KERCHIEFS
SPOOFS
PROOFS
TURFS
DWARFS
PIANOS
SOLOS
CAMEOS
PHOTOS

Page 153

BRONCOS	NPN
CHIEFS	NPN
NPN	NPN
PROOFS	STAFFS
SPOOFS	NPN
SURFS	PIANOS
NPN	NPN
NPN	SOLOS
NPN	CAMEOS
GOOFS	KERCHIEFS

Level 25

Page 158

1. ADMINISTRATOR	13. INVESTIGATOR
2. ADVERTISER	14. LABORER
3. AUTHOR	15. MANUFACTURER
4. BOOKKEEPER	16. OCULAR
5. CALENDAR	17. OPERATOR
6. CONSUMER	18. PARTICULAR
7. CONTRACTOR	19. PECULIAR
8. COUNSELOR	20. REGISTRAR
9. EMPLOYER	21. SIMILAR
10. GOVERNOR	22. SINGULAR
11. GRAMMAR	23. SPECTATOR
12. INTERPRETER	24. TREASURER

Pages 158 & 159

(INTERPRETER)	BOOKKEEPAR	(SPECTATOR)
INTERPRETAR	(BOOKKEEPER)	SPECTATER
INTERPRETOR	BOOKKEEPOR	SPECTATAR
GOVERNER	LABOROR	TREASURAR
(GOVERNOR)	(LABORER)	(TREASURER)
GOVERNAR	LABORAR	TREASUROR

CONTRACTAR
CONTRACTER
(CONTRACTOR)

AUTHAR
AUTHER
(AUTHOR)

ADVERTISOR
(ADVERTISER)
ADVERTISAR

EMPLOYAR
EMPLOYOR
(EMPLOYER)

(PARTICULAR)
PARTICULER
PARTICULOR

SIMILER
(SIMILAR)
SIMILOR

MANUFACTUROR
(MANUFACTURER)
MANUFACTURAR

CONSUMAR
(CONSUMER)
CONSUMOR

(CALENDAR)
CALENDER
CALENDOR

(OCULAR)
OCULER
OCULOR

ADMINISTRATER
ADMINISTRATAR
(ADMINISTRATOR)

OPERATAR
OPERATER
(OPERATOR)

(INVESTIGATOR)
INVESTIGATER
INVESTIGATAR

(COUNSELOR)
COUNSELAR
COUNSELER

REGISTRER
(REGISTRAR)
REGISTROR

PECULIOR
PECULIER
(PECULIAR)

GRAMMOR
(GRAMMAR)
GRAMMER

SINGULOR
(SINGULAR)
SINGULER

Page 160

REGISTRAR
OCULAR
SPECTATOR
BOOKKEEPER
LABORER
CONSUMER
INVESTIGATOR
SINGULAR

PECULIAR
CONTRACTOR
GOVERNOR
ADVERTISER
TREASURER
ADMINISTRATOR
COUNSELOR
PARTICULAR

CALENDAR
AUTHOR
INTERPRETER
EMPLOYER
MANUFACTURER
OPERATOR
GRAMMAR
SIMILAR

Level 26

Page 164

THERMAL <u>THERMal</u>

AGONY <u>AGONy</u>

THERMOS <u>THERMos</u>

STATIC <u>STATic</u>

STATUS <u>STATus</u>

THERMOSTAT <u>THERMoSTAT</u>

ANTAGONIST <u>antAGONist</u>

CYLINDER <u>CYLinder</u>

TRICYCLE <u>triCYCLe</u>

EMPATHY <u>emPATHy</u>

MONOSYLLABLE <u>MONOsyllable</u>

BICYCLE <u>biCYCLe</u>

SYMPATHY <u>symPATHy</u>

MONOTONOUS <u>MONOtonous</u>

THERMOMETER <u>THERMometer</u>

MONOTONY <u>MONOtony</u>

PROTAGONIST <u>protAGONist</u>

Page 165

1. AGONY

2. ANTAGONIST

3. BICYCLE

4. CYLINDER

5. EMPATHY

6. MONOSYLLABLE

7. MONOTONOUS

8. MONOTONY

9. PROTAGONIST

10. STATIC

11. STATUS

12. SYMPATHY

13. THERMAL

14. THERMOMETER

15. THERMOS

16. THERMOSTAT

17. TRICYCLE

Page 166

GIANT GYRO MACHINE

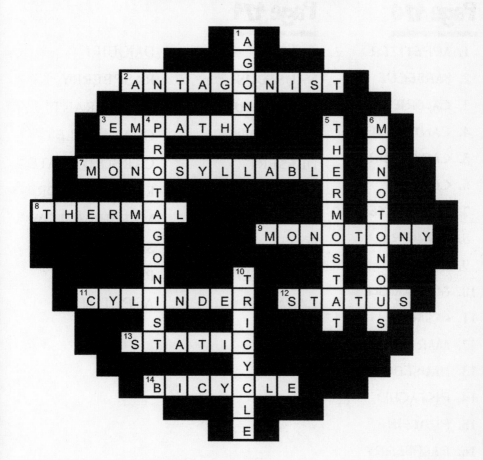

Level 27

Page 170

1. APPETIZER
2. BARBECUE
3. CALORIE
4. CANTALOUPE
5. CARBOHYDRATE
6. CELERY
7. CHOCOLATE
8. DAIQUIRI
9. DESSERT
10. GUACAMOLE
11. LASAGNA
12. MARSHMALLOW
13. NAUSEOUS
14. PISTACHIO
15. PROTEIN
16. RASPBERRY
17. REFRIGERATOR
18. RESTAURANT
19. SANDWICH
20. SHISH KEBAB

Page 171

CELE̲RY
NAUS̲EOU̲S
CANTAL̲OU̲PE
PISTA̲C̲HIO
DES̲S̲ERT
SHI̲SH KE̲BAB
BARBE̲C̲UE
CAL̲O̲RIE
CHOC̲O̲LATE
LASA̲G̲NA

DA̲IQUIRI
RASP̲BERRY
RESTAU̲RANT
GUACAMOLE̲
CARBOHY̲DRATE
REFRIGERA̲T̲OR
MARSHM̲A̲LLOW
SAND̲WICH
PROTE̲I̲N
AP̲P̲ETIZER

Page 173

SHOPPING CART

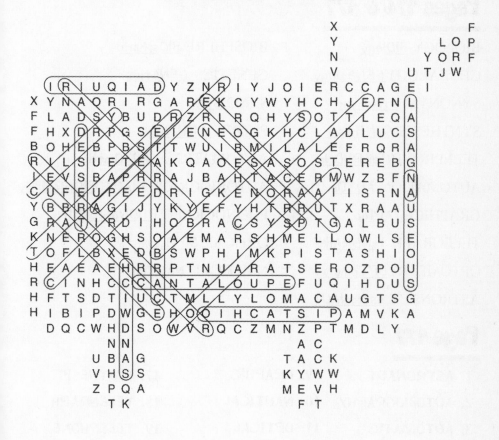

Level 28

Pages 176 & 177

BIOLOGY BIOlogy

BIOSPHERE BIOsphere

GENEALOGY GENEalogy

GENETICS GENETics

SYNONYM SYNonym

SYNC SYNc

SYNTHESIS SYNthesis

PHONICS PHONics

TELEPHONE telePHONe

AUTOMATIC AUTOmatic

AUTOMATION AUTOmation

AUTOBIOGRAPHY AUTOBIOGRAPHy

GRAPHIC GRAPHic

PHONOGRAPH PHONoGRAPH

TELEGRAPH teleGRAPH

OPTICAL OPTical

OPTOMETRY OPTometry

NAUTICAL NAUTical

ASTRONAUT astroNAUT

Page 177

1. ASTRONAUT
2. AUTOBIOGRAPHY
3. AUTOMATIC
4. AUTOMATION
5. BIOLOGY
6. BIOSPHERE
7. GENEALOGY
8. GENETICS

9. GRAPHIC
10. NAUTICAL
11. OPTICAL
12. OPTOMETRY
13. PHONICS
14. PHONOGRAPH
15. SYNC
16. SYNONYM

17. SYNTHESIS
18. TELEGRAPH
19. TELEPHONE

Get Wise! Mastering Spelling Skills

Pages 178 & 179

BIOLLOGY
BIOLIGY
(BIOLOGY)

BIASPHERE
(BIOSPHERE)
BIOSFERE

GENEOLOGY
GENIALOGY
(GENEALOGY)

GENNETICS
(GENETICS)
GENETTICS

(SYNONYM)
SYNANYM
SYNYNYM

(SYNC)
SINC
SYNK

(SYNTHESIS)
SINTHESIS
SYNTHYSIS

PHONNICS
(PHONICS)
PHONIX

TELLEPHONE
(TELEPHONE)
TELLIPHONE

AUTOMATTIC
(AUTOMATIC)
AUTAMATIC

(AUTOMATION)
AUTOMMATION
AUTAMATION

AUTOBYOGRAPHY
AUTABIOGRAPHY
(AUTOBIOGRAPHY)

GRAFFIC
GRAFIC
(GRAPHIC)

PHONNOGRAPH
(PHONOGRAPH)
PHONAGRAPH

TELIGRAPH
(TELEGRAPH)
TELLEGRAPH

OPTOCAL
OPTACAL
(OPTICAL)

OPTOMMETRY
(OPTOMETRY)
OPTOMYTRY

(NAUTICAL)
NAUTTICAL
NAUTYICAL

ASTRONOT
(ASTRONAUT)
ASTRAUNOT

Level 29

Page 182

1. ACCEDE
2. BIRDSEED
3. CEDE
4. CONCEDE
5. EXCEED
6. HAYSEED
7. INTERCEDE
8. PRECEDE
9. PROCEED
10. RECEDE
11. SECEDE
12. SUCCEED
13. SUPERSEDE

Page 183

(SUPERSEDE)
SUPERCEDE

EXCEDE
(EXCEED)

SECEED
(SECEDE)

RECEED
(RECEDE)

PRESEED
(PRECEDE)

(BIRDSEED)
BIRDSEDE

HAYCEDE
(HAYSEED)

INTERCEED
(INTERCEDE)

SUCCEDE
(SUCCEED)

ACCEED
(ACCEDE)

PROCEDE
(PROCEED)

(CONCEDE)
CONSEED

CEED
(CEDE)

Page 185

WORD CEMENTING CHAMBER

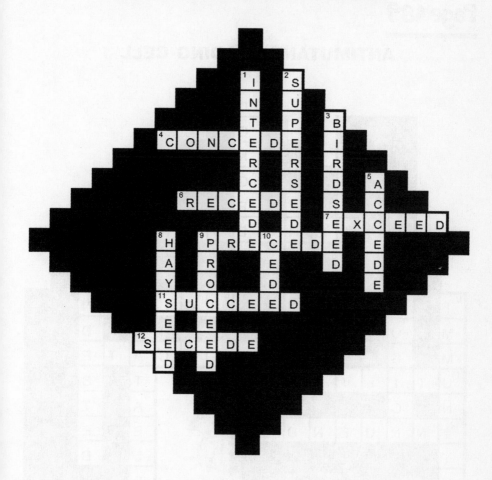

Level 30

Page 189

ANTIMUTANT HOLDING CELL 1

Get Wise! Mastering Spelling Skills

Page 191

ANTIMUTANT HOLDING CELL 2

Level 30 (continued)

Page 193

ANTIMUTANT HOLDING CELL 3

Get Wise! Mastering Spelling Skills

Pages 194 & 195

1. My sisterinlaw claims she's thirtyfour years old but she's been making that claim for as long as I can remember.
SISTER-IN-LAW THIRTY-FOUR

2. Charlie has some of the worst handwriting I've ever tried to read, and I think that's because he's both far-sighted and lefthanded.
FARSIGHTED LEFT-HANDED

3. Which would you rather do: circlenavigate the globe in a balloon or make a trancecontinental trip on a bicycle?
CIRCUMNAVIGATE TRANSCONTINENTAL

4. That guy is so hiperactive that he had to sign up for every intermural sport just so he could burn some energy.
HYPERACTIVE INTRAMURAL

5. It appears that the runaway Russian satelite is on a colision course with our school cafeteria. Bummer.
SATELLITE COLLISION

6. Why is it that guys in movies with metalic teeth always turn out to be the vilain?
METALLIC VILLAIN

7. I would make a terrible politician because I always get panicy when I have to start politicing and speaking in public places.
PANICKY POLITICKING

8. His nose was so zincy from all the sunblock that he smeared on his face that he looked like someone shellaced his nose with plaster.
ZINCKY SHELLACKED

9. The football player ate so many bratwursts that his stomach filled with gasses and his belches sounded like volcanos.
GASES VOLCANOES

Level 30, Page 195 (continued)

10. Which food is used most often in soup, tomatos or potatos?
TOMATOES   POTATOES

11. He thinks he plays concertoes on the pianoes in the music store in the mall, but everyone cringes when he plays.
CONCERTOS   PIANOS

12. I tried to take some photoes of the condoes where we stayed during Spring Break but, just like with every other picture I tried to take, I accidentally left the lens cap on the camera.
PHOTOS   CONDOS

Page 198

ANTIMUTANT HOLDING CELL 4

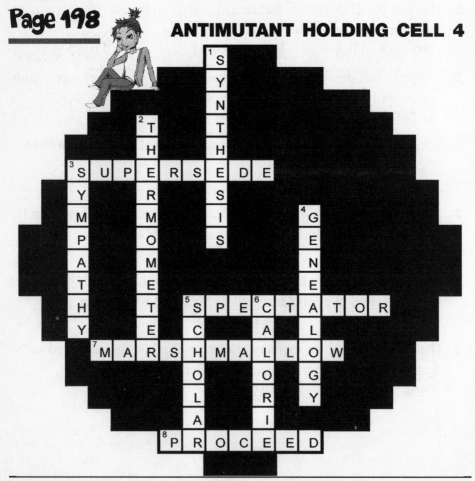